AF575110

A Psalm of Life

The Story of a Woman Whose Life Made a Difference: Willie Lee Campbell Glass

By Patsy Hallman

EAKIN PRESS ★ Austin, Texas

FIRST EDITION

Published in the United States of America
By Eakin Press
An Imprint of Sunbelt Media, Inc.
P.O. Drawer 90159 ★ Austin, TX 78709-0159
email eakinpub@sig.net
www.eakinpress.com

ISBN 1-57168-270-8

9 8 7 6 5 4 3 2

Library of Congress Catologing-in-Publication Data

Hallman, Patsy Spurrier.
A psalm of life: the story of a woman whose life made a difference, Willie Lee Campbell Glass / by Patsy Hallman.
p. cm.
Includes bibliographical references.
ISBN 1-57168-270-8
1. Glass, Willie Lee Campbell, 1910–. 2. Afro-American women—Texas—Nacogdoches—Biography. 3. Afro-Americans—Texas—Nacogdoches—Biography. 4. Nacogdoches (Tex.)—Biography. 5. Glass, Willie Lee Campbell, 1910– —Knowledge and learning. 6. Afro-Americans—Education—Texas—Nacogdoches. I. Title
F394.N32H35 1998
976.4'182--dc21 98-28264
[B] CIP

Mrs. Glass dedicates her book to
the memory of her parents

E. J. and Mary Campbell

and in honor of her friends, students, and colleagues at

Prairie View A&M University
Iowa State University
Texas College
Stephen F. Austin State University
Virginia State
E.J. Campbell Alumni Association
Texas College Alumni Association
Tyler
Nacogdoches
and the
Texas Education Agency

Willie Lee Campbell Glass

Contents

Preface

This is a story of a woman of color who was born into the segregated society that dominated Deep East Texas in the early part of this century. Despite the limitations society imposed, she became a well-educated woman crossing barrier after barrier that divided ordinary people. Today, after almost a lifetime of service, honors come to her from all quarters to testify to the quality of her life and work.

When she was born in 1910, life was almost unbelievably different from life today. Neither of the great world wars had been fought. The automobile was a new invention seen by only a few people, and electricity was found only in cities. The majority of people lived in rural areas where houses had no indoor plumbing or other common amenities used today. Oil lamps provided light, and woodstoves, ice boxes, and rub boards were the normal household appliances. Travel was by horse and buggy or perhaps by train. And people ate only what was raised on local farms.

Life was not easy for people in small towns of America, but for people of color, life was especially difficult. Slavery had been illegal for forty-five years, but a well-defined system of segregation was firmly in place. For example, black people were not allowed to vote or to buy land. Their schools were crude at best. Their destiny in those days seemed to be lives of labor in the service of the white man.

When the two races mixed, the system of behavior was well known by all. For example, black people were required to wait in lines until all whites were served. There were separate entrances to public buildings, separate drinking fountains, and separate waiting rooms. Signs proclaiming spaces and services for "whites only" were everywhere.

The only work available to black people was manual

labor with few opportunities for other work such as teaching in black schools.

Into this world was born Willie Lee Campbell Glass. Despite the hardships and limitations she faced, she accomplished much. The numerous honors and awards bestowed upon her include:

Tyler Citizen of the Year
Texas Women's Hall of Fame
Nacogdoches AAUW Service Award
Meritorious Community Service Award from the City and County of Los Angeles
Delegate to the White House Conference on Aging
United Way of Greater Tyler Community Award
Woman of the Year and Sojourners Truth Award
T. B. Butler Outstanding Citizen Award, Tyler, Texas
Outstanding Alumna, Iowa State University
Negro Hall of Fame, Dallas, Texas
Texas Future Homemakers of America Hall of Fame
Grande Dame of Texas, *Texas Monthly Magazine* Award
Tyler street named in her honor
Nacogdoches Woman's Hall of Fame
AAUW Community Service Award, Nacogdoches, Texas
Philanthropist of the Year, Tyler, Texas
Woman of the Year, Zonta Club, Tyler, Texas
People-to-People Delegation to Scandinavia, Poland and the Soviet Union
People of Vision Award, Tyler, Texas
Sojourner Truth Award
Golden Eagle Award
Key to the City of Los Angeles

This is the story of her life—a life of triumph.

Willie Lee's first portrait, at age three

CHAPTER 1

A Child is Born

Thou are fairer than the children of men; full of grace are thy lips, because God has blessed thee forever.
Psalms 45:3

ON AUGUST 24, 1910, Dr. A. A. Nelson drove his new Model-T Ford carefully over the ruts and holes in the dirt road that led from Nacogdoches to Tyler. Near the northwestern edge of Nacogdoches he reached his destination, for he had come to a neat, spacious, white frame house—the home of the head of the Colored School* in Nacogdoches. Dr. Nelson admired the big, handsome man recently hired to head the school. Earlier, when he learned that a baby was on the way, the doctor had told the man to call him when the time came—he would deliver the baby. The call had come early that morning.

As Dr. Nelson entered the house he met several neighbor women who had come to help, but the woman who seemed to be in charge was a short, strong-looking woman who exuded the very air of confidence. He soon learned that this was the mother-in-law of the schoolmaster. She owned and managed a farm in Cherokee County. Beautiful, light-skinned and strong, she was in charge of the delivery room. She seemed to know what to do, and so did

* Actual name of school for black children in 1910.

Mrs. Missouri Petty, a neighbor and midwife to people in the community. Other neighbor women waiting in the front room soon heard the cry of a newborn. A beautiful baby girl, cut in the mold of her strong, intelligent mother, and her equally strong grandmother, was born on that hot August morning.

In a little while Dr. Nelson was on his way, but when the new father offered to pay for the visit, the doctor replied, "This is my gift to you for the work you do in our town. Bring her in any time she's sick; there will be no charge."

The women, guided by Mrs. Petty, dressed the baby in her first outfit—undershirt, diaper, waistband, baby slip, and a delicate, handmade baby dress. Wrapped in a crocheted blanket, she was ready to be presented to her mother. Mother and father gazed in wonder at this miracle they had created in the plan of the Good Lord.

"She is beautiful," breathed the big man in a whisper.

"The prettiest baby I have ever seen," confirmed the mother.

Later the grandmother recovered the baby and tucked her into a bassinet for her first sleep. The new mother was fed a bowl of broth from boiled onions, and she, too, was soon sleeping peacefully.

When the mother waked and she and the father were admiring their baby, they pondered a name.

"What shall we call her? We only had boy names chosen."

"How about Willie Lee?"

"Good name!"

And so it was: Willie Lee Campbell.

The Campbells were descendants of slaves brought to the Douglass, Texas, area by the Campbell family. The grandfather of this new baby was named Burrell Campbell, a man born of slave parents in Arkansas in 1842. His mother, Nancy, was born in Mississippi. Burrell married Asilee Hackney, and they had three children, Eddie John, Octavia, and Neil. The oldest of the children was Edward John Campbell, the new father.

Early in life heavy responsibility fell on this oldest child—Eddie John or E. J., as he was called. E. J.'s father, Burrell, had a fine, beautiful horse admired by everyone who saw it. Folks said the horse was coveted by many a man, but Burrell would not part with it. One day, two white men arrived at Burrell and Asilee's home and asked Burrell to saddle his horse and help them round up some cattle that had gotten away from them. Happy to help, Burrell saddled his horse and rode away with the men. Neither man nor horse was ever seen again.

Asilee went into such a state of shock and despondency that she died shortly after Burrell disappeared. The children were divided among the kinfolk. E. J. lived with first one relative, then another. For a while he lived in the Upshaw community with his Aunt Ella and Uncle Gus Upshaw.

Uncle Gus Upshaw was a strong, energetic man, and he taught E. J. how to work hard and how to earn money. E. J. often helped at the "Gus Upshaw Fish Trap." This was a business venture that brought Gus the money to buy the farm land he acquired in large amounts. Gus dammed up a portion of the Angelina River that ran by his place and in it he placed a huge fish trap. Every morning it was filled with all kinds of fish. Gus sold them for three cents a pound, and he made quite a bit of money doing that. People came to the "Gus Upshaw Fish Trap" to buy their fish. He peddled some as well. E. J. learned about the value of work and the importance of land ownership while he lived with the Upshaws.

Later he moved to Garrison to live with his aunt and uncle, Albert and Louisiana Mast. The Masts sent him to the Colored School in Garrison, and when he finished the lower grades there they sent him to Nacogdoches to finish the upper grades that were available in town. From the Masts he learned the value of an education.

Wherever he lived he stayed in contact with his younger brother and sister. Through the years he and his own family maintained a close relationship with his sisters and their families.

In Nacogdoches, he attracted the attention of the local state representative. The legislator admired the young man for his determination to learn, for his intelligence, for his sense of responsibility for his younger brother and sister, and for his wholesome appearance. E. J. was six feet, seven inches tall and weighed 250 pounds, but he reacted to people with gentleness and respect. In a day when there was always someone around who wanted to put down any person of color, E. J. seemed to know how to relate with confidence to almost everyone.

When E. J. finished the Nacogdoches school, the local state representative presented him with a scholarship to Prairie View Normal. The tuition for the first semester was $2.50. After one year at Prairie View, E. J. qualified for a teacher's certificate, and he began teaching school back home in the Upshur Community (an area northwest of Douglass). Each summer he would return to college to get a few more courses needed for a bachelor's degree. It was not uncommon in those days for a person to teach for years before completing a degree. For E. J. it was almost forty years; he was finally awarded a B.S. degree in 1933, long after he was a very successful educational leader. That was the same year Willie Lee got her master's at Iowa State. Each year he would attend a summer institute provided around the state for teachers of Negro schools.

One summer, when the institute ended, E. J. married Miss Mary Gertrude Kennedy, one of the young women who had also attended the training. The couple met at the institute that was held annually in Nacogdoches. E. J. drove his buggy to Rusk, and the couple was married on the front porch of the Kennedy home in 1906.

Mary Kennedy was the daughter of an African/Irish family in Cherokee County. Her mother was Lucinda Egbert and her father was Isreal Kennedy. They had farmed in the Rusk, Texas, area since anyone could remember. And they were successful farmers, farming cotton and corn on 210 acres—a large farm for one family to manage in those years before automation. Mary's father developed various illnesses early in his married life, and his wife took over the management of the farm. Mr. Kennedy also worked part-time at a hotel in town.

Mrs. Kennedy was knowledgeable about farming, about managing resources, and about saving. Her successes were reflected in her home. In those days a typical farm home was three, maybe four, rooms. In the front room was the fireplace, a dresser, a rocker, several straight chairs, and two beds. Clothes hung on pegs driven into the wall behind doors. Only the most successful family could afford wardrobes for their clothing. A small room between this front room and the kitchen held two more beds for children. A successful farmer might have a fourth room that was a bedroom across an outdoor hall, or dogtrot.

At the Kennedy home, Mrs. Kennedy wanted to have a sitting room for her children as they grew up and were of an age to have guests. With careful shopping she found a piece of furniture called a "wardrobe-sleeper." It looked like a big wardrobe with a mirror in the center door, but it had another important feature; it was built on heavy rollers, and when swung around on those rollers, a folding bed built into the back of the wardrobe could be lowered for sleeping. With this new piece of furniture, she removed the beds from the front room, and with a new settee and some additional chairs, the family had a sitting room. (This wardrobe-sleeper is currently the centerpiece of the Gallery in the Human Sciences Department, South Building, Stephen F. Austin State University.)

Mrs. Kennedy shared her skills with her children, especially with her daughter, Mary. This eldest daughter was bright, strong, and eager to learn. She was one of the brightest children in the Colored School in Rusk, but in Rusk there was no high school for Negro children. Just when the Kennedys were trying to find a way to get more education for Mary, the Rev. Lawson Reed came to their area to start a Baptist church. He and some of the men in the community put up a brush arbor, and the church began. Before long Brother Reed spotted the bright little

The Campbell Family

Professor Campbell

Mrs. Campbell and Willie Lee

E. J. Campbell home.

girl, Mary Kennedy, and when he learned her family wanted her to go to high school, he offered to take her to Nacogdoches where there was a Colored High School. She would live in the parsonage with him and his wife. (This was not an unusual practice, for the Reverend Reed in his time started fifty-two churches in East Texas, and he and his wife often boarded bright young people from the small communities so that they could get a high school education.)

Mary taught at North Church School and Winter's Hill, while E. J. taught for three years in the Upshur Community before they were hired to teach in the Colored School in Nacogdoches.

In those years, black people were not allowed to buy property, but supporters of the new school leader recognized his importance to the community, and they made it possible for him to have a home. One of the white men bought several acres of land on what is now Old Tyler Road and, for an appropriate sum, deeded the land to E. J. and Mary. There the Campbells built the lovely white frame house where they lived when Willie Lee was born.

Papa always praised everything I did, but Mama kept my head out of the clouds. She said that others with my advantages might have done a lot more than I did.—WLCG

CHAPTER 2

Getting an Education

But lo, thou requirest truth in the inward parts; and shalt make me to understand wisdom.

Psalms 51:6

Willie Lee Campbell started school when she was six months old! Actually, after she was born her mother was able to stay home for several weeks because the Colored School began late in the year—only when the cotton-picking season ended. For a time after Mary returned to her classroom, Grandmother Kennedy helped care for the baby. But by the time Willie Lee was six months old, E. J. and Mary worked out a plan to take her to school with them each day.

There was no such thing as a daycare for Negro children in Nacogdoches, but Mary was a resourceful woman. Each day she packed all the baby's needs in a knapsack, wrapped the baby in warm blankets, and carried her to school riding on the front seat of the family buggy. The family made a handsome sight as they drove from the west part of town to the east side where the Colored School was located. The big, strong, handsome man drove the neat little buggy pulled by two good horses. Beside him, riding with pride and dignity, was the beautiful young woman holding the baby.

When they began the trip, Mr. Campbell lit his pipe and enjoyed smoking as they made their way along the road into town. But as they neared downtown, he always extinguished the smoke and put the pipe in a can on the floor of the buggy. White folks didn't like to see "coloreds" smoking.

The couple were as regular as clockwork in their trips to and from school. Other black people watched their progress across town with great pride, and white people watched with respect, seemingly grateful for this model of excellence in their community.

At the school Mrs. Campbell fashioned a baby bed-playpen made from straight-back chairs. Placing them seat-to-seat, she tied the legs together, and with a big pillow on the seats, Willie Lee had a comfortable bed. When the pillow was removed, she had a safe place to play. Of course, there were always plenty of children ready to play with the baby.

Early on, Mrs. Campbell identified one young student with special care-giving ability, and she became the chief babysitter. Her name was LuElla Thorn, and she had a continuing relationship with the Campbells until her death in the 1990s. They provided a home for LuElla and her family throughout her life.

COLORED SCHOOLS

Schools for Colored People in the early part of the twentieth century were, at best, inferior to whatever the local white school was; at worst, they were a shame to all who called them educational institutions. In Nacogdoches the Colored Schools were made better by the Campbells.

At the time of the Campbells' appointment to the Nacogdoches Colored School, the entire system consisted of one four-room building with 125 students. The year before they began teaching in the Colored High School, there were only five graduates—all girls.

E. J. Campbell School

Dr. Nelson

Willie Lee's babysitter, Mama Lou.

The Campbells saw at once that they could make a difference. Their goals included improving the physical plant, improving the curriculum, developing new programs, and taking leadership roles in the community.

With E. J. Campbell's leadership, programs were developed in home economics, agriculture, manual training, and health. For extracurricular activity, Professor Campbell promoted organizations for drama, debate, the sciences, and civics. A Black Dragon athletic organization fielded teams in all sports. A marching band and an orchestra completed the new programs. Eventually, drivers' education was also added to the curriculum.

Professor Campbell taught mathematics, and Mrs. Campbell taught history. Each of them held high standards for academic excellence. Alumni of E. J. Campbell High School are quick to point out that graduates of the school were well grounded in basic subjects. One man said, "Professor Campbell knew that math so well, he could be looking out the window, and if you made a mistake on a problem you were working on the board, he would say, 'No, no, my boy, that's not the answer,' and he would show us the correct solution."

Alumni point to case after case of successful graduates of E. J. Campbell High School. Clarence McMichael said, "My own mother was a graduate of that school in 1910, and after she finished Bishop College, she was immediately employed as a tutor by a wealthy family in California; they wanted the best for their children, and they knew with her background, that's what they were getting!"

Mrs. Campbell not only taught history but also was head of the school's athletic program. She went to all the football games and often fed the team around her own kitchen table. One of those former players said, "I can still see the spread of food Mrs. Campbell would lay out for us. There would be everything you can think of to eat for the main meal, then three or four kinds of cake—coconut, chocolate layer, and angel food!"

The man went on to say that the Campbells worked

hard to get uniforms for the team. Sometimes there were second-hand ones available from the Nacogdoches High School, and occasionally Stephen F. Austin College provided them with their teams' discarded uniforms.

The Campbells ran a tight ship. The school was organized for student achievement—for individual development. No misbehavior was tolerated. Professor Campbell believed preventive discipline was the best kind. Within the classrooms, girls sat on one side of the room, and boys sat on the opposite side. Similarly, at recess, boys played on one side of the playground and girls on another.

Getting more physical space for the school was not easy, and it was especially difficult for Professor Campbell to persuade the board that the school needed an auditorium. Finally, he implemented a new strategy. Each time the white superintendent of schools came to the Negro campus, Professor Campbell announced a chapel service. He packed children into the only room available for an assembly. There would not even be standing room for all the children and teachers. Then he would ask the superintendent, and any others who came with him, to speak. After a few of those crowded chapel services, the board voted funds for an auditorium—a first for a black school in East Texas.

With similar strategies, Professor Campbell was able to get the road by the school paved. For years it was a dirt road, impassable during rainy weather. One rainy spring, Professor Campbell invited the local state representative to speak at commencement. Sure enough, the rains came, and as the representative's car started up the hill, it stuck in the mud. He climbed out and waded up the hill to give his speech. Soon afterward the road by the school was paved.

When discussing Professor Campbell's strategies with the interviewer for this story, Charles D. Williams, an E. J. Campbell alum, said to Clarence McMichael, "Don't forget how he always fed the school board 'round about budget time. Those were fine meals!"

Despite the leadership of the Campbells, the black school suffered from inequities—hand-me-down books, many teachers without certificates, limited resources, and high dropout rates. The concept of "separate but equal" was a false one, even in Nacogdoches.

Historian Ralph Steen, former president of Stephen F. Austin State University, said in his *Texas History* (1948): "As a general rule the educational policies of the state apply to Negro as well as to white schools, but in many cases the Negro schools are less well-equipped and operate for shorter terms. About half of the schools for Negro children are one-teacher schools. . . . generally speaking the Negro in the country lives on the poorest farms, in the poorest houses, and under most objectionable sanitary conditions." It was, of course, children from these homes who filled the Campbells' classrooms.

Francis Edward Abernethy, professor of English, writing an E. J. Campbell biography that appeared in the *Daily Sentinel* (1985), said this about the times in relation to schools and schooling for Negro children:

> One reads the stories of E. J. Campbell's days and studies the record of that time and suffers a shame and an embarrassment. Those who talked about "separate but equal" school facilities during the early days of desegregation were using words without meaning. There was nothing approximating equality in the school system. And we accepted it all because we were conditioned to that being the way it was.
>
> We have seen great things in our lives—cures for diseases that had killed and crippled millions, scientific advancement to the point of putting a man on the moon, wars won and wars lost—but nothing has occurred in the United States in this century as historically and socially important as the breaking down of the legal barriers that separated the black and white races.

ELEMENTARY SCHOOL

By the time she was five years old, the Campbells decided Willie Lee was ready for first grade; after all, she had been absorbing the curriculum for years. She could read and do all sorts of other activities of the first and second graders.

On the first day of school, she marched right up to the first grade teacher's desk and said, "I already know how to spell."

"Really," replied Mrs. Curl, "can you spell a lot of words?"

"Of course," said the confident little girl. "I can spell Willie Lee Campbell and I can spell Nacogdoches. And Papa said that anyone who can spell Nacogdoches can spell anything!"

Mrs. Curl became the favorite of all Willie Lee's elementary schoolteachers, probably because the two got off to such a good start when Mrs. Curl responded positively to the little speller.

It was not difficult for Willie Lee to rise to the top of her class, even in the first grade. She was to continue that tradition of excellence and superiority through high school, a bachelor's degree at Prairie View, and a master's at Iowa State.

Of course, there was no lunch room or cafeteria in the Colored School. Everyone brought a sack lunch. Mrs. Campbell packed a basket each day for her family, and at lunch time Willie Lee went to "Papa's office" to get her food. She then carried it back to her room, where she often shared it with other kids whose lunch was not so appealing. Her ham sandwiches and fried chicken legs looked much better than the sausage biscuits, or worse yet, butter biscuits, that many children brought for their only lunch day after day.

Willie Lee and the other children read from a *McGuffey's Reader*. Each story included a moral lesson. Here is one story she came to love:

> Once upon a time, there were two frogs who lived in a road ditch beside a farmer's barn. One day when the farmer did not get enough milk from his cows to fill the milk can, he took a bucket and reached into the ditch of

water beside the barn and poured a bucket of the water into the milk can. The farmer was unaware that two little frogs were in the water. He simply put the lid on the can and lifted it into his wagon and set out on his rounds to sell the milk.

When those frogs were caught in that big milk can they didn't know what to do. The first little frog said, "Let's kick." And so they began. They kicked and kicked and kicked. They got awfully tired and finally the second little frog said, "I cannot kick any longer." So he gave up and sank to the bottom of the milk can.

But the first little frog kept kicking, even though he was very tired. He kicked and kicked and kicked until something wonderful happened. His kicking made a ball of butter in the milk, and when it did, he hopped upon the butter ball and rode along comfortably until the farmer stopped at the first house. When the farmer took the lid off the milk can, the frog jumped out and hopped away to his home in the pond.

Willie Lee may not have seen the true moral in the frog story at the time, but she was accustomed to strategizing at an early age in order to get her own way. For example, one day her father was upset about problems at work and his patience was in short supply by the time he got home. That was the very day Willie Lee chose to do something he had asked her not to do, and he decided to spank her. When she discovered his intent, she ran from him. He followed in hot pursuit as they raced around the yard. Willie Lee glanced over her shoulder and saw that she would soon be caught, so she stopped and quickly turned around to face her father, saying, "Papa, don't come another step. I'm tired of this game!" Her statement so disarmed her father that he couldn't do anything but laugh. Of course, that saved Willie Lee from the intended punishment.

Willie Lee has always been quick-witted and able to think on her feet. Her track record of successes began early in life as she programmed herself for success. Early on she refused to accept failure as a possibility. When her schoolmates in grade school would forget their speeches, she would crawl under her desk in embarrassment.

Even today she is a very cautious risk-taker. She leaves nothing to chance. Planning and careful preparation of every detail for any event in her life is an integral part of her lifestyle. Although her friends tell her that she must be prepared to accept some failure in life, she retorts, "I can't help it. I just can't stand failure!"

HIGH SCHOOL

The "champion attitude" Willie Lee possessed in the elementary years was even more fierce during high school. She was active in the drama club, on the debate team, and in girls basketball. She loved to learn, but her favorite subject of all was history. She longed to be just like her history teacher, Miss Molly P. Quinn. She determined to make history her major in college, and to become a teacher like her parents. Even as a child, when she and her friends played "school" she insisted on being the teacher. "Mama said that was being selfish, that I ought to share," she related later.

Willie Lee remembers one debate she won during high school where the young men debated the point: "Who should be educated if a family could not afford to educate both girls and boys?" One male debater summed up his argument by saying the male should be educated because he will be the head of the household and will make all major decisions, to which Willie Lee quickly retorted, "The female should be the one educated because it is true that the males might be the head, but the female is the neck and turns the head wherever it wants the head to go!"

At the Colored School, the basketball team was very important. With her height and energy Willie Lee was a natural for the team. But to her utter chagrin, her father insisted she wear a hat to protect her from the cold of the outdoor courts. No one else wore a hat, and Willie Lee was totally embarrassed to wear one. It did look peculiar paired

Willie Lee in uniform

with the uniform of the time—long bloomers and a middy blouse. After a while she learned a strategy for getting rid of the despised hat. This is what she did. After she was on the court, when she would see her chance to get the ball and make a goal, she would toss the hat to a friend on the sideline. Then, catching the ball, she would race down the court and throw the ball into the basket. When she made the points, Papa didn't fuss about the abandoned hat.

Papa and the whole community took great pride in the winning team. Willie Lee says that in the four years she was on the high school team, they never lost a game.

In high school Willie Lee's self-esteem, self-worth, and self-confidence blossomed. Among the factors that contributed to her self-image and leadership abilities were her opportunities to be so often in the company of successful adults because of the Campbells' professional life. She developed leadership in the family when she assumed the "boss" role with younger cousins.

Willie Lee's schools years in Nacogdoches were successful, but not always happy. Sometimes the other kids called her a "little rich girl." After all, they said, she was different from them. She had parents who could give her anything she wanted. And besides that, she had friends that none of the other teens could claim as their friends—Dorothy Davis, the daughter of the white school superintendent, and Julia Nelson, the daughter of the white doctor. Willie Lee suffered such snide comments about her friends and her status in the community, but she responded as her parents taught her—without anger and in ways to build an even larger network of friends.

During her senior year, Willie Lee was named "Miss Nacogdoches" and later valedictorian of her class. On the night she was to give the valedictory address, R. F. Davis, superintendent of schools, was unable to attend because he was hospitalized for an illness. He sent word for Willie Lee to come to the hospital the next day and repeat the speech for him. She obliged with pride in herself, her school, and her family.

PRAIRIE VIEW A&M

A high school graduate at seventeen, and valedictorian of her class, Willie Lee went directly to Prairie View A&M. Most graduates of the Colored School in Nacogdoches who went to college chose Prairie View. That was probably because each year Professor Campbell took interested students and their parents by train to visit the campus. The train left early and all the high school students gathered at the station to see the seniors leave.

Prairie View A&M University, the second oldest public institution of higher education in Texas, was created by the Texas Constitution of 1876. Having already established the Agricultural and Mechanical College of Texas (later to be named Texas A&M University) in 1871, legislators pledged in the Texas Legislature of 1876 that "separate schools shall be provided for white and black children, and impartial provision shall be made for both." On August 14, 1876, the legislature established the "Agricultural and Mechanical College of Texas for Colored Youth" and placed responsibility for its management with the board of directors of the Agricultural and Mechanical College at Bryan.

Classes began March 11, 1878, with the original curriculum designated as that of a normal school to prepare and train colored teachers. The curriculum expanded to the arts and sciences, home economics, agriculture, mechanical arts, and nursing after the Hatch Act of 1887.

When Willie Lee arrived at Prairie View in 1927, enrollment was considerably more than the 500 students who studied there at the turn of the century, and the student body included the best and the brightest among the young black students of Texas. In 1919 the university had become a four-year senior college.

Later, in 1937, master's degree programs were added, and in 1945 the name was changed from Prairie View Normal and Industrial College to Prairie View University, and in 1947 the legislature changed the name to Prairie View A&M College of Texas. In 1973 the present name was determined by the legislature: Prairie View A&M University.

Today university enrollment exceeds 6,000, including more than 1,000 graduate students. Since 1981, students of all races are welcome at Prairie View. Students come from throughout the United States as well as from many foreign countries.

Prairie View is dedicated to excellence in teaching, research, and service. Although its mission is to serve Texas through high quality undergraduate, graduate, special/continuing education and research programs, its service area extends to the nation and the world. The university is committed to cultural diversity, equal opportunity, and to meeting the needs of a diverse society and the priorities of Texas. It is a state-assisted institution, a land-grant institution, and a "statewide special purpose" institution by legislative designation.

For her move to Prairie View, her parents bought Willie Lee a fine big trunk. In it they placed the best wardrobe they could buy or have made for Willie Lee. The wardrobe was typical for college girls in 1927. It contained a navy chiffon dress for formal occasions, a white embroidered linen for parties, a wool suit for church, five new fall dresses, and various other necessary items. There was a gym suit, and a fine long wool coat. The clothes came from the best dress shop in Nacogdoches, Mayer and Schmidts. Or they were made by the best seamstress in town, Cassie Dunagan.

Willie Lee's college wardrobe also consisted of one more outfit—one from Neiman-Marcus of Dallas, the ultimate in women's clothing stores. She was able to have the Neiman's outfit because her two best friends, each a couple of years older than she, joined in the preparations for sending Willie Lee away to college. The girls were Dorothy Davis, the daughter of the white school superintendent, and Julia Nelson, the daughter of the doctor who delivered Willie Lee.

"When our Willie Lee goes away to college, she should go in style," announced Dorothy Davis to her friend Julia.

"Indeed she will," agreed Julia. "Let's see that she has at least one outfit from Neiman's!"

It was not difficult to persuade their parents to join in the project, and soon the three girls were on the train from Nacogdoches to Dallas to make the purchase. And that's how the little black girl from a small town in Texas went to college with the best of everything.

Years later a professor at Iowa State questioned her about how she was able to afford a college education.

"Did you have a scholarship?"

"No."

"Did you have a white benefactor?"

"No."

"Well, how did you manage to get here?"

"My parents paid my tuition and all my expenses," replied Willie Lee with the pride and confidence her parents had long ago built into her personality.

At Prairie View she majored in home economics. She had gone there to study history, but soon after she arrived, the president of the college, W. R. Banks, addressed the female students in an assembly. He said that home economics was an up and coming field, that its teachers would make more money than other teachers, and that it was a federally supported program that was being put into all schools.

"Who," he asked, "will consider this new field of study?" Willie Lee, along with dozens of others, raised her hand.

At that time the home economics curriculum placed heavy emphasis on food preparation, food sanitation, and sewing. Each student was required to hand sew a layette as well as develop skills at the sewing machine. Each participated in classes designed to teach them formal dining and elaborate service at receptions, coffees, teas, and similar social gatherings.

The women in her family—her professional mother and her resourceful grandmother—had already helped her to develop a refined sense of style, but the years at Prairie View emphasized the principles that have guided her good taste and personal presentation for life. When she graduated in 1931, she was once again the top honor graduate.

IOWA STATE UNIVERSITY

The Campbells always wanted the best for Willie Lee, and she set high goals for herself as well. So it was no surprise that she wanted to continue her education with graduate study. But where to go? It was 1931, and in Texas only white students were allowed in universities. Again, Campbell resourcefulness and networks surfaced. Mrs. Hunter, the local black extension agent, was a family friend, and through her the family learned that Iowa State University had a fine graduate program in home economics and would take a black student. The Campbells immediately made arrangements to send Willie Lee.

Iowa State University of Science and Technology was established in 1858. Located at Ames, Iowa, it is a land-grant institution long recognized for programs of excellence in agriculture, design, business, family and consumer sciences, engineering, and veterinary medicine. Today it also has an institute for atomic research. In 1923 the university admitted one of its first black graduate students in home economics—Willie Lee Campbell from Nacogdoches, Texas.

Because she was not allowed to live in a dormitory (which were only for white girls), Willie Lee's parents found a boardinghouse that would take her. When she arrived in Ames, the situation looked bleak. Loneliness and isolation appeared to be prime features of her time there. As winter arrived and the snows came, so did Willie Lee's feelings of being misplaced.

At Prairie View she had established the habit of writing letters each week to her parents—separate ones to her mother and father. She continued the practice in Ames. One Sunday when she was especially discouraged she wrote to each parent, and to each of them she wrote this line in the letter:

> This place is not for me; everything and everyone here is white; the students are white; the professors are white;

> shopkeepers are white; the buildings are white; the clouds are white; even the ground is white with snow! I want to come home.

Each parent responded to that week's letter. Her father's letter contained $80, enough money for a train ticket to Nacogdoches, and his letter said, "Catch the first thing smoking." Her mother's letter said, "Look in the mirror and you will see someone who is not white; you can make it!" And she did.

Dr. Nelson joined Mrs. Campbell in employing strategies to keep Willie Lee in Iowa. Once when she was discouraged she wrote that she was ill and needed to come home to see Dr. Nelson. The doctor replied to her, "Willie Lee, if you are really sick, I will come up there." Of course, Willie Lee replied that she was feeling better and Dr. Nelson need not come. She was later to say, "I could not fail because I did not want to, and because my parents and the people in Nacogdoches were depending on me to be successful."

After that early discouragement, Willie Lee set her course to complete the master's at Iowa State. It was not easy. Some black students who entered Iowa State soon failed and went home in disgrace. Willie Lee knew she could not let that happen to her. A professor once asked her to take the class for a day and to use the class period to review a particularly important book by Paul Popenoe, *Modern Marriage,* for the other students. Mrs. Glass said she spent every waking moment studying that book between the day of the assignment and the reporting day. As she walked between library and classroom and to her place of lodging, she practiced her comments. "Every tree on that cinder path knew my report," she exclaimed.

In 1933 she received the master's degree from Iowa State University. She was one of the first black women to complete the graduate program and the youngest person to receive a master's degree from the university.

Later, Willie Lee studied at a variety of other institutions. She completed graduate work at Columbia University, New York; Union Theological Seminary, New York; and the University of Wisconsin, Madison.

Achieve excellence without excuse.—E. J. Campbell

CHAPTER 3

E. J. Campbell Family Life

They that sow in tears shall reap in joy. He that goeth on his way weeping, and beareth forth good seed, shall doubtless come again with joy, and bring his sheaves with him.

Psalms 126: 6-7

The Campbells were busy people, and they lived lives of purpose and service. They were committed to taking care of themselves and their family, while at the same time they were committed to careers that lent excellence in education in the community. To reach those goals they knew they must get as much education as was possible for each of them to obtain. They also knew they must work extra hard at their jobs as teachers and educational leaders. One of their peers said, "With education, hard work, good judgment, and plenty of people skills, the Campbells excelled in everything they did."

Their energies did not stop with their paid employment, for they used Saturdays and summers to work on their family farm, thereby increasing the family resources. And always, they were involved with community activities. Members of the St. Paul Christian Methodist Episcopal Church, they each assumed lifetime leadership roles in their religious community.

The Campbells also recognized the necessity of financial resources and the power of money. Toward that end they worked hard at their paid employment, did additional work to make their farm a paying venture, and had an almost religious devotion to saving.

Willie Lee tells a funny incident that illustrates both her father's commitment to saving and his concern for others. The story related to Professor Campbell's attempt to teach other adults the value of saving.

At the time, Professor Campbell was called simply "Professor" by most people, and by his black peers the name was often shortened to "Fess." One year when the cotton crops promised a good yield, Professor Campbell spoke to one of his cousins about saving. He said, "When you sell your cotton, go downtown to the Stone Fort Bank and put some of your money there for safekeeping; it's the only way you will ever get ahead."

The man looked skeptical and asked, "Can I get it anytime I want it?"

"Of course you can," replied Professor Campbell.

When the cotton was sold the cousin carried $15 to the bank. Weeks passed, and one day, Professor Campbell looked up from his desk at school to see him rushing into the building with a worried look on his face.

"What's the trouble?" asked Professor Campbell.

"Fess," he said, "I went for some of my money and the man at the window in the bank said there is no money for me there. You said I could get it out anytime. You said it would be safe!"

"Now, hold your horses," replied Professor Campbell. "I'll go to the bank and see what the problem is. Meet me there at 11:30."

True to his word, Professor Campbell drove to the bank. When he inquired about the problem, he learned that the man had told the banker to put his money with Mr. Campbell's rather than to set up his own account! Soon the matter was rectified, and the bank gained a regular customer.

Both Mary and E. J. had been taught the value of land, and in two different ways they acquired many acres. First, they continually added to their acreage in Nacogdoches as land became available next to their property. And second, as each of her brothers and sisters decided they were not interested in the Kennedy land they inherited, Mary bought their part of the home farm. Thus, at her parents' deaths, Willie Lee inherited large tracts of land in both Cherokee and Nacogdoches counties. By that time surveyors had discovered that the Cherokee County land was rich in minerals, making it even more valuable than Mary had imagined as she was accumulating it.

Soon the Campbell farm lands grew large enough to require helpers, and E. J. built farm houses, leasing land to sharecroppers. The families worked the land for a share of the profits. The landowner furnished the land, a house for the family to live in, seeds, and farm equipment, and the sharecropper furnished the labor.

After World War I, the Campbells were able to trade their horse and buggy for a car. They chose a small Buick. One of E. J. Campbell's students said, "It was one of the first cars I ever saw—had those curtains at the windows—it was before the time of cars with glass windows. How proud we students were to see our school leader in that fine vehicle!"

As Willie Lee was growing up, she was her father's constant companion. When he went to the bank, she went along; for that matter, she went all over town with him as he conducted business and participated in community events. They were a common sight in Nacogdoches—the big tall black man and the well-dressed little girl, hand-in-hand. As a small child she caught the eye of the president of Commercial Bank, E. I. Sturdavant, and each time she and her father went to the bank, Mr. Studavant gave Willie Lee a quarter. Early on, she learned that a smile and a courteous greeting to the president paid off. She kept her quarters in a Calumet baking powder can.

She found other ways to accumulate change too. As Willie Lee and her father rode to check the progress of the cotton crop and see the farmers, she would hop out of the wagon and open the gate to each field. To reward her,

Professor Campbell gave her a nickel each time she remembered to offer help. The baking powder can grew heavy with coins. In the fall, when the cotton was sold, her parents gave Willie Lee all the buffalo nickels they had saved during the year as her share of the profits from the cotton crop.

Her mother insisted that the quarters and nickels be saved. By the time the coins in the baking powder can reached $15, the Campbells told Willie Lee she could open her first bank account. She made her deposit in the Stone Fort Bank, and to this day she keeps an active account there.

Shortly after the first deposit, Willie Lee asked her parents for a new pair of Bilickin shoes. Her mother replied, "We do not have any money to spare for shoes right now, and besides, you don't need new shoes." Willie Lee promptly said, "Mama, I'll lend you enough money from my account to pay for the shoes if you will pay me back."

At that offer, Mr. Campbell, who was listening in on the conversation, said, "I believe I have enough extra cash for the shoes without borrowing any."

Willie Lee then overheard her mother say to her father, "It's ridiculous for you to train her that way!" But the shoes were forthcoming.

As Willie Lee grew older and could manage her own money as an adult, her mother's advice came back to her: "Keep some money in every bank in town—money is power."

Later her father was to emphasize to her the value of savings, the power of money, and the need to always be prepared. He would say, "Willie Lee, never leave to go anywhere without money in your pocket for train-fare home!"

Willie Lee became frugal with her own spending. She tells of a time in her adult life when a relative asked for a loan of $600. After a discussion with the person, Willie Lee was convinced that there was no intent to repay the loan, so Willie Lee suggested she would help the relative get the loan from a local bank. The relative said, "Oh, no, no . . . I do not want to do that because they will make me pay interest."

"I'll pay the interest," replied Willie Lee. After all, she reasoned, Papa always said, "Be very cautious about lending money; banks, not people, are lending agents."

NO FEELINGS OF DISCRIMINATION

Willie Lee seems to have lived a privileged life as the only child of a successful, well-educated family. She says, when asked, that she never felt discriminated against. However, as she muses about the past, one story surfaces over and over in the memories of her childhood.

It was not long after World War I, around 1920, and in those days of separation of the races it was dangerous for Negroes to say anything derogatory about any community program. At that time, the Red Cross was a prominent cause, and people from all walks of life contributed to it. There were well-organized community drives to collect for the Red Cross, and Professor Campbell headed the drive in the Negro community.

There was among the black businessmen a man whom people described as very strange; he was unpredictable, quick to anger, and always carried a gun at his side. When Red Cross drive time came, Papa said to the community committee, "Let me approach Lem Wooding [not the man's real name]; don't any of you other fellows mention it to him."

Notwithstanding Professor Campbell's request, two white men approached Mr. Wooding and he responded with much cursing and the statement, "Damn the Red Cross!"

The men left, but they reported the incident downtown and immediately two policemen said they would take care of Lem Wooding! Away they went to Mr. Wooding's business, and as they approached, shooting broke out with one of the policemen hit. Lem Wooding ran.

The whole town was closed while men searched for

Wooding, but he was nowhere to be found. A lynch mob was formed and the horde of angry men went first to the home of Wooding's brother. Despite the fact that the brother was old and walked with a cane, he was shot and killed when he couldn't tell them where Lem was hiding. His wife was tied to a tree, questioned, and left to die. Neighbors cut her loose when the white men moved on.

Mr. Wooding had another brother, and he was brought to the Campbells' house for safekeeping until the mood of the town was quieter.

Days later, the word went out that Wooding had been found and brought in to the jail. Papa was called to town to identify him. Everybody was saying, "It's him, it's him!"

"No it isn't," said Papa after he looked at the man in jail. "A person might change the color of his hair or other things about himself, but he can't change the shape of his head. It isn't Lem Wooding." (Later they found out the old fellow in question was an escapee from the Rusk State Hospital.)

Wooding was never found, but the white man who killed his brother was brought to trial. Willie Lee, who went everywhere with her father, was allowed to attend. Only ten years old, she was in awe of the prosecutor. The man knew the times, and he knew how to approach the jurors. In his closing statement he said, "Gentlemen, I won't ask you to punish this white man for killing poor old Uncle Elick; I wouldn't ask you to do that, no sir; I wouldn't even suggest that white jurors convict a man who killed an old black. But gentlemen, if you don't find him guilty, you need to tear down this courthouse and burn the jail, you may as well dismiss law and order in this town!" In only a short time the jurors were back with a verdict of guilty, and the man was sent to prison.

Another incident frightened Willie Lee almost as much as the Lem Wooding episode. It happened that a black man on foot ran into a buggy driven by a white woman. The woman's brother was so angry about the accident that he put out the word he would kill the man who caused the accident said his sister was traumatized by the shake-up. Town leaders feared another racial incident. The black man had to be hospitalized because his leg was broken in the accident, and Dr. Nelson called Papa about ways to minimize the tension. They decided what to do. They simply put a "NO VISITORS" sign on all entrances to the hospital, and kept the man there for a few days until the mood of the town changed.

HOME CHORES

When she was growing up, Willie Lee had specific home duties. Both her parents taught her to work, but her mother was much more insistent about the chores than her father was. In fact, he often quarreled with Mrs. Campbell about the need for Willie Lee to do so much work.

Mary's response was always, "We don't know how long we will live, and she has to learn to be independent."

As was common at the time, the Campbell kitchen had a wood cookstove. And, as with all farm families, the job of bringing in the stovewood was the children's. Willie Lee said, "I started bringing in the stovewood when I could only carry it one stick at a time."

Another regular chore she had as a child was to keep the hot water reservoir on the cookstove filled. It held fourteen gallons of water, and to the child, it seemed as if it was always empty.

As Willie Lee grew older, Mary taught her to cook and gave her specific baking responsibilities. On Saturdays, when her parents went to the farm to work, Willie Lee was left at home to bake and to help the housecleaner, Mary Molandes.

Each week when Willie Lee had her cake baked she would cut it and give a piece of it to Mary Molandes to take home for her dessert. On one particular Saturday, as they worked together, Mary Molandes mentioned to Willie Lee that she had never had a whole cake. As the work continued Willie Lee made a plan, and when Mary Molandes was ready to go home, she presented her with a freshly baked cake—all of it—to take home to her family.

When her parents came in from the farm, Willie Lee related the story.

"What made you give away *all* the cake?" asked her mother.

"I just wanted them to have, for once in their life, what we have every week," was the reply.

Without a word, Mrs. Campbell set about cooking supper, and Mr. Campbell said, "It's all right, little girl; I'll fix it," and he drove to the local bakery and bought a cake to replace the one she had given away.

Willie Lee said, "My favorite chore of all my home tasks was cake baking. I loved to bake big beautiful pound cakes and give them to our friends. I gave away so many, they began to call me the 'cake girl.' I still enjoy giving cakes to my friends. It gives me great pleasure." Here is the recipe Willie Lee uses.

MILLION DOLLAR POUND CAKE

1 pound real butter
3 cups sugar
6 eggs
1 teaspoon lemon juice
1 teaspoon vanilla
4 cups sifted cake flour

Cream butter and sugar until the mixture is smooth and creamy. Add eggs, lemon juice, and vanilla, and beat well. Add sifted flour and beat gently until flour is folded into mixture. Bake in greased and floured stem pan for 2 hours at 300 degrees. Cool for ten minutes; remove from pan.

Mary was a good cook, and the Campbell family ate well. Each day when the family returned from school, Mary prepared their supper. Usually it was some form of fried meat, maybe hash, and whatever vegetables were available from the farm. Baked sweet potatoes, mashed white potatoes, field peas, turnip greens, tomatoes, onions, hominy, corn—all the southern foods were on the Campbell table.

For a quick supper, Mary often made hash and to accompany it she prepared "cush." This old-fashioned dish resembled the boxed stuffing sold in stores today.

On Sundays the family had a fine big Sunday dinner with fried chicken or cured ham served with "lady peas" and mashed potatoes. The dessert was usually cake accompanied with whatever fruit was in season. A favorite was pound cake topped with peaches folded into thick country whipped cream.

For snacks Willie Lee's favorite were syrup cookies. She said that for as long as she can remember her mother had a cookie jar full of them, and there was never a better cookie! Mrs. Campbell's syrup cookies were so famous that an old man interviewed for this story remembered how good they tasted when he ate them as a high school football player. He said, "She always used sorghum syrup; it makes the best cookies!"

Here is the recipe from Mary Campbell's kitchen:

SYRUP COOKIES

2 cups sugar
2 eggs
½ cup molasses
Pinch salt
1½ cups shortening
4 cups flour
2 teaspoons soda
1 teaspoon each ginger/cloves/cinnamon
¾ cup buttermilk

Mix; shape into balls. Place on greased cookie sheet; press with a fork. Bake 10 minutes at 350 degrees.

On a summer day, Mary often set Willie Lee to churning. The big crockery churn with the wooden dash held five gallons of cream, and it took a lot of churning to make butter. Willie Lee said, "It was the most boring job I ever had.

Even though I couldn't carry a tune, I would get a songbook and with it in my lap, I would sing every song in the book before the butter came. I hated churning so much that with the first check I got when I started teaching in Virginia I bought an electric churn and sent it home."

"Oh," responded the interviewer, "you bought your mother a churn."

"No, I bought it for myself, so that when I went home, I would never have to churn again!"

There was another chore that Willie Lee hated nearly as much as churning. That was washing dishes. At home, with only three people in the family, the chore wasn't so bad, but when they visited the extended family in Rusk, it was an awful chore which usually fell to the girls.

Once when the family was on its way to visit the Rusk family, including the grandmother and all the aunts, uncles, and cousins, Willie Lee complained to her parents that she guessed she would spend her days washing dishes.

"Now, Willie Lee, it isn't becoming of you to complain. You must be a cheerful helper when we get to your grandmother's no matter how many people there are to eat," responded her mother.

Later, in an aside, E. J. said quietly, "Willie Lee, here's a handful of change; use it to pay some of the other girls to do your part of the dishwashing and you find something else to do." And so she did.

"You'd be surprised how many dishes one of those country girls would wash for a nickel," she recalled.

LEISURE TIME

Willie Lee loved horseback riding. She had her own horse, named Redbird. He came only to her call, and he was her faithful courier for all of her teenage years.

Besides riding her horse, Willie Lee spent her leisure time visiting. The Campbell family often visited Mary's family in Rusk. There on Grandmother Kennedy's farm was a large house with plenty of space for all the aunts, uncles, and cousins. Grandmother was prepared to feed all who came. At times the smokehouse would be filled with as many as fourteen smoked hams. Sausage was stored for the year's use in great crockery churns. As a part of the hog-killing process in early winter, sausage was made and then an enormous number of the sausage patties were fried. These were then placed in the churns in layers with melted lard from the fat, rendered during the hog-killing, poured over each layer. All through the winter, sausage was available for the country-style breakfasts served in the big kitchen.

There was always plenty of fresh milk, cream, and butter on the farm. To keep it and other perishables fresh, the food was lowered into the well. There, in buckets at depths of 100 feet or more, it stayed cool and fresh.

Professor Campbell, who loved to hunt, especially liked to hunt quail. He frequently came home from a bird hunt with a sack full of birds. That meant the family could have a fine meal of smother-fried quail, with hot biscuits and cream gravy and tall glasses of iced tea. It was good eating!

BANISHED TO AUNT ALICE'S

In 1918 there was a serious outbreak of diphtheria in Nacogdoches, and families who could do so sent their children to stay with relatives in other towns. Willie Lee was sent to Aunt Alice's in Rusk. "What an experience," she said. "At home, I could eat whenever I was hungry. If I wanted to eat something between meals there were cookies, fruit, or other things available, and I was free to select what I wanted at any time. But at Aunt Alice's things were different ! There was *no* eating between meals. You ate your meal, and there was nothing else until the next meal. I was so distressed by this that I wrote at once and told Papa about it.

"Can you believe what Papa did? He sent a case of

peanut butter and a case of crackers on the next train to Rusk! We children ate peanut butter snacks all summer; it was wonderful!"

VISITING THE RELATIVES

There were many opportunities for the Campbells to be with relatives, and the cousins were important in Willie Lee's life. She was a leader among them. For example, once when the cousins were staying with Grandmother Campbell for an extended time during the summer, each was assigned a household chore. One of the most difficult chores was cleaning the lamp chimneys, and someone was assigned to do that each weekend.

On one particular Saturday, the assignment fell to cousin Leonard Kennedy. He carefully washed all nine lamp globes and set them out to dry on the back porch wash-shelf. He felt satisfied as he looked at that row of sparkling clean glassware! But just as he turned to empty his pan of wash water in the nearby flower bed, he heard the horrifying sound of breaking glass. Turning to look, he saw that a chicken from the yard had flown into the row of lamp chimneys, knocking them onto the ground. Several were broken.

Leonard was wrought with fear of telling his grandmother what had happened. As he stood petrified with fear, Willie Lee came to the rescue. "We can fix them so no one will notice," she said. And quietly and meticulously, the children glued the glass pieces together into a whole. Then they carefully set the globes back on the lamps; only one was seriously damaged and it was placed on the mantel with the broken side to the back. No one was to tell what had happened.

That very evening as the family gathered in the front room after supper, Grandmother Kennedy moved to stand by the fireplace as she talked with the family. As she did so, she placed her arm on the mantel. Instantly the mended globe fell off the lamp and broke into many pieces. She was struck with awe at how a simple touch of the mantel had caused the lamp globe to break!

"If I had not seen this with my own eyes I would not have believed it," she exclaimed.

"Oh Grandmother I saw it too . . . unbelievable. I'm glad I didn't break it," said Leonard Kennedy.

To the day of her death, many years later, no one ever told the lady the true story of the lamp globes.

COTTON PICKING

Willie Lee had learned the value of hard work, but there were a few times when she wished she had been able to skip it. She described her experience with cotton picking.

"Most of my friends picked cotton during the fall, and one year I decided I wanted to do that too. Papa said cotton picking was work for the people on the farm, but I wanted to try it. I was envious of all the money my friends were making in the fields. They said they made enough money during the cotton picking season for all their spending money during the winter.

"Now there was a cotton field across the road from our house, and I asked the man who owned it if I could pick for him. He agreed and Papa bought the heavy ducking used for making cotton sacks. Mama sewed a sack for me on her sewing machine. It was about eighteen inches wide and six feet long. A wide strap held it on my shoulder.

"Picking cotton was the hardest work I ever did. Walking down those rows, leaning over to pick the cotton from those prickly burrs, and pulling that heavy sack was awful. After a short while, my back felt as if it would break. That summer was so hot that we had days and days of 100-degree weather. Finally, Papa said it was just too hot for me to be in the fields. I had made $14 and that ended my cotton-picking career. [Today the cotton field where Willie

Lee began and ended her "cotton career" is a fine productive watermelon farm managed by Clarence McMichael, a former student of the Campbells.]

"Papa did let me work every year at the Normal Institute. It was usually held at Zion Hill Baptist Church and I was the "water carrier." I had to draw water from the well and carry a bucket and dipper to each class. With the heat of an East Texas summer, those teachers drank lots of water!"

CHURCH

Willie Lee fondly remembers the religious side of her family life.

"Church was always a part of our lives. The first memory I have of a church service was Great-grandmother Nancy's funeral. It was in a tiny little church building in the Upshaw community. We all sat crowded together on benches as the preacher held that service. I had a sore throat and Mama had painted my neck with iodine because that was supposed to be good medicine for colds. I wore a little white suit, and I had to hold a handkerchief between my neck and the collar of my new suit to keep the iodine off my new white coat.

"I remember seeing that little church many times as I was growing up. It was a little shot-gun building with homemade, crude benches for seating. It was torn away a few years ago and now the community has a nice building."

E. J. Campbell served as a steward in the Methodist church, and the family was active in the local congregation. The religious instruction Willie Lee received as she was growing up served her well when she became the wife of the president of a church-related college. One of the roles she assumed was fund-raiser, and she did that very well. In the many presentations she gave over the years for alumni, community leaders, and potential donors, she made generous use of the scriptures. Her theme in the presentations was most often "service," and she likened the service she was calling for to the service promoted in Christian philosophy. Jesus' command to Peter, "Feed my sheep, feed my sheep, feed my sheep," was frequently quoted by Willie Lee in her speeches.

To this day Willie Lee Campbell Glass maintains an active relationship with the Nacogdoches congregation.

E. J. CAMPBELL AND THE COMMUNITY

The Campbells' family life was greatly influenced by the role of E. J. Campbell in the Nacogdoches community. He was highly respected by the white community, where he was often called as a mediator between blacks and whites. One person interviewed about Mr. Campbell said, "He saved many a black from going to jail. If a person got in trouble with the law, he called Mr. Campbell first. He would work with the sheriff and try to find a solution for the person—try to get him back to work and keep him out of jail."

Because Mr. Campbell believed so strongly in an education, he encouraged many Nacogdoches students to go to college. He would talk to the students and parents, assuring them that college was a possibility for them. Then each year he organized a "college trip." He arranged for prospective college students and their parents to take a train ride to Prairie View A&M, where they toured the campus and met with advisors. He went with each group year after year; it was a treasured event for E. J. Campbell High School students.

As a result of his work with the people in Nacogdoches, Mr. Campbell was loved by many. One man who was interviewed said:

"My father loved Mr. Campbell so much that he would do anything for him. For example, my father, who lived in the Upshaw community which is twenty-one miles from Nacogdoches, would ride his horse all the way into Nacogdoches to bring Mr. Campbell an opossum when he caught a good fat one. Mr. Campbell loved roasted opossum, so my father would bring him one every few months during the fall and winter. He would catch the opossum, skin it (sell the skin for its fur), and ride his horse, Dan, to Nacogdoches with his gift to Mr. Campbell. Mrs. Campbell would chill the meat overnight, then roast it the next day. Along with sweet potatoes and turnip greens, it was good eating."

Professor Campbell died in 1937. An interesting measure of the respect that the white community held for Mr. Campbell was seen at his death. There have always been mortuaries for whites and separate ones for blacks in Nacogdoches, and when Mr. Campbell died, no one had ever heard of either group sharing the services. But at his death, the Cason Monk Funeral Home (white) called the family home and asked if Mr. Campbell could lie in state at their funeral home. The Campbell family graciously accepted the gift as a tribute to Mr. Campbell. On the day of the funeral, all black schools in the county were closed so that people could attend the services.

Mrs. Campbell lived for many more years. Actually, her life as a widow may have been a busier life than her life as a teacher and homemaker in Nacogdoches, for she moved to Tyler to join the Texas College staff. There she served for many years as dean of women and as a dorm mother. Alumni say that the team of the president (Willie Lee's future husband), Mrs. Glass, and Mrs. Glass' mother was a powerful one. "If you want to get something done," they said, "go to one of them!"

Mrs. Campbell worked at Texas College until her death in 1964.

Professor and Mrs. Campbell are buried in the Cleaver Cemetery on Butt Street in Nacogdoches.

He inspired the people of a country. He brought hope to those enslaved in ignorance, and poverty. From the corn fields of Douglass to the halls of justice and knowledge, his inspiring presence radiated hope and emancipated his people from the shackles of ignorance. From the river banks of the Angelina to the dome of the state capitol he added dignity to the land and to the people, and made us proud to be Americans.—From the biographer of E. J. Campbell

Chapter 4

Building the Glass Image

You shall eat the fruit of the labor of your hands; you shall be happy, and it shall be well with you.

Psalms 128:2

The Campbells taught their daughter many things—to work hard, to get all the education she could get, to save, to find something good in everyone, to be honest in all her transactions, and to approach life in a positive way. But nothing they taught her was any stronger than the lesson of networking. Day after day, as the little girl followed her father around town—to work, to the bank, to the white school superintendent's office, to the grocery store, to church, and to their own sharecroppers' cabins—she saw the results of a network of friends and acquaintances.

Each evening as she overheard her parents discuss strategies for improving the school, for making more money on the farm, or for giving her the best life possible, she absorbed the lessons of working with people to reach personal goals.

One of the people who was most important in helping the Campbells prepare Willie Lee for the good life was Mrs. M. E. V. Hunter, an extension agent for a large area of Texas that included Nacogdoches. Mrs. Hunter was a person of color—tall, with high cheek bones, and straight black hair. She may have been a descendant of both Native

Americans and African Americans. Mrs. Hunter often stayed with the Campbells when she visited Nacogdoches.

As the time approached for Willie Lee to finish Prairie View, she and the family began to seek a college where she could do graduate work. Colleges and universities all over Texas were approached, but in every case they were turned away. No home economics program in Texas would take a person of color into their graduate program.

Home economics was a major program at Stephen F. Austin State Teachers College in their own town—in Nacogdoches—but its doors were closed to Willie Lee and to all people of color. No amount of good relations with the leaders in Nacogdoches, no amount of good will among them, and no amount of appreciation for the work of the Campbells in the community affected the situation. Negroes could only attend schools for "coloreds" in the Texas of the first half of the twentieth century.

"I don't know what we are going to do," worried Professor Campbell as he talked one evening to their guest, Mrs. Hunter. "She must go on with her education, but no one will take her."

"Send her to Iowa State," Mrs. Hunter advised. "They will not want her—they want no persons of color, but they will have to take her. I went there as an undergraduate, and now they have a few Negro undergraduate students. I'll make the contacts for you."

With Mrs. Hunter's help the family approached Iowa State, and Willie Lee was accepted. Later when she was near graduation with the master's degree, offers came from many places, but again, the influence of Mrs. Hunter directed Willie Lee's choices.

VIRGINIA STATE

Willie Lee Campbell was a valuable person—a rare one in the United States—for she was a Negro woman with a master's degree. Prior to World War II, that was almost unheard of. In fact, researchers say that in all the country few blacks held graduate degrees.

Offers from Howard University and her alma mater, Prairie View, were attractive, but Willie Lee chose Virginia State. By this time, Mrs. Hunter had taken the position as head of the Home Economics Department at Virginia State, just outside Washington D.C., and she wanted Willie Lee on her faculty.

Virginia State University was founded in 1882 as the Virginia Normal and Collegiate Institute. In 1920 the land-grant program for black students was moved from a private school, Hampton Institute, where it had been since 1872 to Virginia Normal and Industrial Institute. In 1923 the name was changed to Virginia State College for Negroes.

The university is situated in Chesterfield County at Ettrick, on a bluff across the Appomattox River from the city of Petersburg. Virginia State has a long history of outstanding faculty and administration. In the first academic year, the university had 126 students and seven faculty (all of them black), one building, thirty-three acres, a 200-book library, and a $20,000 budget.

Today the university is fully integrated, with a student body of 50,000, full-time faculty of 250, and a library of 200,000 books. Its campus covers 236 acres with an accompanying 416-acre farm. The annual budget is $31 million, exclusive of capital outlay. Its mission is to provide a comprehensive university for the Commonwealth of Virginia. It promotes academic programs that integrate instruction, research, and service. Ultimately, the university is dedicated to the promotion of knowledgeable, perceptive, and humane citizens—secure in their self-awareness, equipped for personal fulfillment, sensitive to the needs and aspirations of others, and committed to assuming productive roles in a challenging and ever-changing global society.

To this, America's first fully state-supported four-year institution of higher learning for black students, Willie Lee Campbell came for her first professional role.

At Virginia State Willie Lee's assignment was to teach

quantity food preparation, methods of teaching home economics, and home management. She soon developed a teaching style that would produce excellence in her students wherever she taught.

An interviewer once asked, "Miss Campbell, what did you tell your students that made them so successful?"

"I started every course, regardless of which one it was with these instructions," she responded, and listed:

- Be on time to class. Even if your culture is time-relaxed, you must be on time if you want to succeed.
- Work hard. You may have to work twice as hard as a white person, but you can do it. Hard work pays.
- Develop a positive self-concept. Find something you can do well, and work to develop that talent. Everybody can be good at something.
- Deal with each individual with respect. Everybody is someone special.
- When you have a task before you, learn all you can about how to do it well, then practice, practice, practice. Leave nothing to chance; prepare yourselves to perform with excellence.
- Act with confidence; when you know how to do something well, you have no need to be fearful or self-conscious!
- Study, read, observe, practice.
- Be careful of your appearance; cleanliness, careful grooming, and appropriate dress create an image of a professional.

A VISIT FROM MRS. ROOSEVELT

About the same time Willie Lee graduated from Iowa State and began her career in Virginia, the country elected a new president. The Republican president, Herbert Hoover, had presided over the White House during the time of the greatest depression the United States had ever known. Now, in 1933, there was a ground-swell to elect a new man to lead the country. The Democrat, Franklin D. Roosevelt, was chosen as the new president.

Willie Lee and her fellow professors went to Washington for the inauguration. She remembers that every state in the union had a band that performed on the White House lawn on that cold day in January. After the music, the inauguration ceremonies began. First, President Hoover made a speech, then came Mr. Roosevelt. After contracting polio in 1921, Mr. Roosevelt never walked again, but he was seldom photographed in his wheelchair. Mrs. Glass remembers that for the inauguration, his sons rolled the chair onto the lawn where the speeches were made. Then, at the appropriate time, the sons helped him to the podium, and standing on each side of him, balanced his body while he took the oath of office and made his inaugural address in a standing position.

The Roosevelts were a strong, proud, and resourceful family, and one of the most able and most resourceful of them all was the president's wife, Eleanor Roosevelt. Shortly after the Roosevelts moved into the White House, Mrs. Roosevelt began what was to become a great service to the president and to the nation, for she began visiting people all over the country. President Roosevelt said that Eleanor was his eyes and ears to the people.

One of Mrs. Roosevelt's first visits was to Virginia State University. Not only was she interested in the welfare of the whole country, she was one of the first national leaders to highlight the needs of African Americans. Visiting Virginia State, a Negro college, was one way she began this effort.

As soon as the college president knew Mrs. Roosevelt wanted to visit the campus, he contacted Mrs. Hunter, the head of the Home Economics Department, to ask if the students in the Home Management House would host the First Lady for a dinner at noon on the day of the visit. Mrs. Hunter readily agreed and called in Willie Lee, who was director of the House. Of course, Willie Lee agreed to have her girls prepare and host the dinner, but Mrs. Hunter was so concerned that everything be perfect that Willie Lee said she made everyone a nervous wreck. In later years she was to say, "I was very comfortable with Mrs. Roosevelt; it was Mrs. Hunter who made everyone feel pressured and inadequate!"

Miss Campbell and her students began at once to plan for the big day. They chose a menu, planned the flowers, and practiced cooking each dish until it was pronounced "just right." They also practiced speaking to the First Lady. Willie Lee described the preparations to her parents:

"We had Mrs. Hunter over to taste each dish—several had to be adjusted to meet her standards. We cleaned and polished the entire Home Management House—even the closet shelves. Then we began to practice meeting and talking to our guest. As we practiced, I played the role of Mrs. Roosevelt. The girls practiced answering the door, asking her to have a seat, offering her a beverage, announcing the dinner, talking during the dinner, and visiting afterwards in the living room. I made questions on every subject I thought she might introduce, and the girls practiced answering them. Still we were nervous, because everyday Mrs. Hunter came to inspect and to warn us that we could make no mistakes!

"At last the week arrived, and the Good Lord took a hand—Mrs. Hunter was called away from the campus, leaving us to manage the visit without her. What a relief! With her out of the way, my girls' confidence returned, and everything worked out beautifully.

"At the stroke of twelve, Mrs. Roosevelt arrived in a chauffeured limousine. She was dressed in a navy blue suit and hat. People have asked me if she was an attractive lady in person. I can only say that her personality was so lovely, we thought she was beautiful. She was caring, concerned, genuine, intelligent, respectful—a lady in every way. During the dinner, and afterwards in the living room, she talked to the girls about their families, asking where they were from and what their parents did back home. She asked each of them to tell her what they would like to be doing in four years. By the time the dinner was over, the girls were comfortable enough to not only answer her questions but to query her as well. She told them about life in the White House and about Mr. Roosevelt's dreams for the country.

"We began the meal with a consommé, then followed that first course with chicken and dressing, giblet gravy, string beans, white potatoes, congealed salad, and hot rolls. The dessert was apple pie topped with homemade ice cream. (The girls at Virginia State made the best homemade ice cream in the world.)

"As the years have passed and the historians have written so much about the Roosevelts, I have read that Mrs. Roosevelt gave little consideration to food in the White House—that she would simply order the cook to bring in a tray of tuna sandwiches and glasses of iced tea when she had a guest. If that is true, then she must have really enjoyed the dinner my students served to her! None of us will every forget it!"

The recipe for the famous ice cream follows:

HOMEMADE PEACH ICE CREAM

(Like that made by Mrs. Glass' students at Virginia State)

1 quart of mashed peaches made from fresh, fully ripened peaches
3 cups of sugar
6 whole eggs, beaten
1 quart thick cream
1 tablespoon vanilla
Enough whole milk to fill a one-gallon ice cream freezer to the 2/3 full mark

Blend the sugar and peaches and let set for several hours. Combine the peach/sugar mixture with beaten eggs, vanilla and cream and pour into freezer can. Add the required amount of whole milk. Fill the ice cream freezer bucket with alternate layers of ice and salt, and crank until the mixture is stiff. Remove the dasher and pack the ice cream in additional salt and ice for one hour before serving. Serve in chilled bowls.

SOCIAL LIFE

Not all of Willie Lee's life in Virginia was work. She made friends with many other young professionals and had an active social life. The group loved to play cards and travel. On weekends they returned to Washington, D.C., or traveled to New York City and other points of interest in the area.

When Willie Lee told her parents about the New York visit, her father wrote at once with this advice: "I've heard about the part of New York called Harlem—stay away from it at all costs!"

A handsome young male professor soon began to court Willie Lee. Dr. Cannon was from New Jersey, and when Willie Lee wrote home about him, both her parents were frightened. Said Mrs. Campbell to one of her friends, "My heart chilled to the bone; what if Willie Lee marries this man and never comes home again? Can you imagine her living in New Jersey?!!!"

Maybe that fear contributed to the parents urging her to take a year's leave of absence and come home to Nacogdoches for a year when she suffered an illness during the third spring of her Virginia experience. Or maybe Willie Lee was just homesick. After all, there was no doctor in all of Virginia that would give her the care and attention that their own Dr. Nelson would.

After a rare telephone call to her parents, and permission to take some time off from her teaching duties, Willie Lee went home to Texas.

BACK HOME IN NACOGDOCHES

Soon after Willie Lee returned to Texas she was hired at her own high school to teach home economics. She applied the same high standards to high school teaching that she held at the college level, and the home economics program at E. J. Campbell High School got off to a good start.

But soon Willie Lee's attention was divided, for as the year began, her friend Mrs. Harris introduced her to the man she was to marry, and the year was filled with courting as well as with teaching.

CHAPTER 5

Courtship and Marriage

My beloved spake, and said unto me, Rise up, my love, my fair one, and come away. For lo, the winter is past, the rain is over and gone; The flowers appear on the earth; the time of the singing of birds is come, and the voice of the turtle dove is heard in the land. . . . Arise, my love, my fair one, and come away with me.

Song of Solomon, 2: 10-13

The man Willie Lee Campbell married was Professor D. R. Glass, president of Texas College in Tyler, Texas. President Glass was born Dominion Robert Glass in 1890 in Forsythe, Georgia. Educated at Atlanta University and at Harvard, he was recruited to come to Texas to serve as the registrar at Prairie View A&M. It was actually at Prairie View that Willie Lee first met him, but they knew each other there only as professor and student. In fact, Professor Glass served as the class sponsor for Willie Lee's class.

"I thought Professor and Mrs. Glass were nice people. I respected them as I did all my professors," said Willie Lee, as she reflected on her first acquaintance with Mr. Glass.

Several years and many experiences passed between Willie Lee's first acquaintance with Mr. Glass and their later courtship. First there was completion of her program of study at Prairie View. Then came the years at Iowa State. Next the years of teaching at Virginia State, and finally a year back home in Nacogdoches. During that time the first Mrs. Glass died.

Actually, Willie Lee came home to Nacogdoches after three years of teaching in Virginia because she was not well. When her father learned she had been sick for several weeks, he insisted she return to Nacogdoches immediately. The faithful Dr. Nelson was called in to make a diagnosis.

"Is she seriously ill?" asked the father.

"No, no, E. J. The girl is just run down—needs her mother's cooking and a lot of that pampering you are famous for. Why don't you let her teach in your high school this year?"

And so it was decided. By the end of the summer Willie Lee was feeling like herself again, and she began the fall as the home economics teacher in the Nacogdoches Colored High School. While she was away, E. J. had persuaded the school board to provide vocational labs for the school, and a home economics teacher's position was available. It worked out just fine.

As the year progressed, Willie Lee renewed acquaintances with many of her high school friends. One friend in particular proved to be the catalyst for her life to come. Tory Harris was a friend from high school, and now she was the wife of the black dentist in Nacogdoches. Their paths had separated when Willie Lee went to Prairie View and Tory went to Texas College. Now they were both living in Nacogdoches again.

"Willie Lee, I want you to meet our Texas College president," proposed Tory soon after they renewed their acquaintance.

Oh, thought Willie Lee, *she's trying to get me a job in Texas—probably in cahoots with Mama and Papa.*

Nevertheless she agreed, and the Harrises arranged for a dinner party at their home.

At the dinner Willie Lee and President Glass were seated beside each other. As the evening progressed they had an opportunity to talk.

"Miss Campbell, do you smoke?" the president asked.

"Oh, no."

"Do you ever drink alcoholic beverages?"

"No," she replied, and seeing where the conversation was heading, she added, "But I do love to play cards!"

President Glass pondered that for a few minutes, and Willie Lee thought, *This is a strange interview for a job!*

Then, to her amazement, she heard him say, "Miss Campbell, am I too old to go out with you?"

Willie Lee was shocked speechless, but presently she did mumble something that eventually resulted in another dinner invitation.

Later, when she related the strange turn of events to her parents, her mother said, "How old is he?"

"I don't know."

"You didn't ask him? Why not?"

"I was so shocked I couldn't think what to say or ask."

Papa knew what to say. "Well, you just write and tell him you appreciate his friendship but you have considered your situation and have decided you cannot see anyone just now. After all, you are still recovering from your illness."

"Now, Mr. Campbell," Mama interjected, "let's think about this. Maybe she could just go one time to see if she likes him."

After more discussion, Papa was persuaded, and he and Mama agreed that Willie Lee would keep the dinner engagement. Papa was not happy about it. In fact, he felt the same way about this that he felt about all the boys she had known. "Not one of them is good enough for Willie Lee!" he believed.

On the appointed evening, President Glass arrived in Nacogdoches in his new Dodge, driven by his own chauffeur. It was a pleasant evening, and as a result more dinner dates followed. They were either at the Harrises or at the Campbells because there were no restaurants available to Negroes in Nacogdoches.

PRESIDENT GLASS

Willie Lee learned a lot about Mr. Glass. He was a brilliant man, well-educated, conservative, and a true gentleman. Reared in Georgia, he now considered his home to be in Ohio, where his parents had moved soon after he went away to college. A man of small stature, he was always impeccably and formally dressed.

His first wife had died from injuries incurred in a train accident during the time when Willie Lee was teaching in Virginia. They had no children.

As his successes at Prairie View became known across the state, he was recruited as president of Texas College. He was to serve in that role for thirty years.

As the courtship continued Willie Lee came to respect "Mr. Glass" a great deal, and Mama persuaded Papa that it would be a good match.

"If we break this up," she reasoned, "she may marry that Dr. Cannon who she's been dating in Virginia. Then where will she be? New Jersey—that's where! We'll never see her more than once a year if she's way up there. With this man, at least she will be close to home."

And so Mary convinced Mr. Campbell that Mr. Glass was right for Willie Lee. And in due time, Willie Lee decided he was too.

THE PROPOSAL

One evening after a grand dinner in the Campbell dining room, the couple sat together on the front porch, and Mr. Glass proposed. Willie Lee accepted with what Mr. Glass reported was the dignity of a lady and the sureness of his beloved. Mr. Glass had a fine diamond engagement ring ready for the occasion.

After the appropriate visit with her parents, the preparations for the wedding began. With both families prominent in two East Texas towns, there was no doubt that the wedding would be a special one—and a large one.

As the year progressed the plans were made. Willie Lee and her mother went by train to Houston to buy her trousseau. At Foleys they found a Mrs. Richardson heading the bridal department, and before long they discovered she, too, was from Nacogdoches.

"Don't worry about a thing, my dear. I know just what you need," said Mrs. Richardson, and she set out to help the mother and daughter put together the perfect trousseau. A formal white wedding gown, a second-day dress, a going-away dress, lingerie, and all the appropriate accessories were bought. When all the choices were made, Mama was satisfied that her daughter would be the perfect bride.

THE ANNOUNCEMENT

The following engagement announcement appeared in local papers:

> Mr. and Mrs. E. J. Campbell, Nacogdoches, Texas announce the engagement of their daughter, Willie Lee, to Dominion R. Glass, president of Texas College of Tyler, Texas. The wedding will take place during the month of August. Mrs. Floy D. Price will attend Miss Campbell as matron of honor. Miss Helen Elizabeth Kennedy, as maid of honor and Misses Jewel and Juanita McBroom as bridesmaids. G. N. Redd of New York City will attend Mr. Glass as best man. Bishop R. A. Carter of Chicago, Ill., will perform the ritual.
>
> Miss Campbell is a graduate of Prairie View State College, Prairie View, Texas, and Iowa State College, Ames, Iowa, and has attended Columbia University. She has taught in the Virginia State College and the Nacogdoches City Schools. She is a member of Alpha Kappa Alpha Sorority.
>
> Mr. D. R. Glass is a graduate of Atlanta University, graduate student of Harvard University, Cambridge, Massachusetts, and is now President of Texas College, Tyler, Texas.

THE WEDDING

Mrs. Campbell engaged Mrs. Reavley to direct the wedding. The Reavleys were longtime white Nacogdoches residents. They lived in a big house on Mound Street where Mr. Reavley was something of an entrepreneur. In fact, he made the first potato chips sold in Nacogdoches—cooked them in the family kitchen. Later Mrs. Reavley headed the food service for the Nacogdoches schools. (Their son Tom Reavley is now an associate justice of the U.S. Circuit Court in New Orleans.)

Mrs. Reavley made the cake, arranged the flowers, engaged the musicians, and helped the family plan for a lovely outdoor, afternoon wedding. The invitations were mailed, and according to Professor Campbell's report, "Everyone came, and brought someone with them."

It was a gala occasion with the formal ceremony in the garden of the Campbell home on Old Tyler Road. Willie Lee's bridal gown of embroidered silk was a full length gown with lace insertions and seed pearl motifs. The long train was chiffon net. Bridesmaids wore pastel organdy dresses with matching bonnets. Each carried a bouquet of roses. The best man and groomsmen wore summer-white suits. The tiny flower girls were dressed in pantaloons and the accompanying ring bearer was in a white tuxedo.

In order to accommodate the large number of guests invited to the wedding, an altar was fashioned under a trellis at the front garden gate. The white picket fence that surrounded the house made an enclosed area for the bridal party, with the guests standing on the large lawn beyond the fence. Trellis and picket fence were entwined with greenery and white blossoms. Baskets of additional flowers enhanced the outdoor altar.

Seven hundred and fifty guests attended the wedding, coming from Nacogdoches, Tyler, Rusk County, Prairie View, Austin, and indeed the entire state. After the ceremony, a reception was held on the lawn. Guests were served cake and punch from bridal tables set up under the big trees.

D. R. Glass, beloved husband.

A sketch of the wedding dress

The following news article appeared in local papers:

Nacogdoches, Texas, August 27. In a ceremony performed by the Right Rev. Randall A. Carter, Bishop of the Third Diocese of the Colored Methodist Episcopal Church, Miss Willie Lee Dorothy Campbell, daughter of Mr. and Mrs. E. J. Campbell, became the bride of Mr. Dominion R. Glass, of Tyler, Texas, and Atlanta, Georgia. The ceremony took place on the lawn of the Campbell residence, at 6:30 o'clock in the afternoon.

Miss Doris Novel, pianist, played the accompaniment for Dr. Lattimore's solo. Dr. Lattimore is a cousin of the bride.

The bride who was escorted to the exquisite altar arranged on the southeast corner of the lawn, entered on the arm of her father. She was gowned in a lovely bridalring satin dress, made on empress lines. A soft neckline was draped high at the throat, and the sleeves, loose sleeves above the elbows, fitted to the lower arms and tapered to points above the hands. A veil of illusion followed the lines of the train, falling from the halo headdress of illusion, which was made with scallops of tulle, which dipped to a point in the center. She carried a bouquet of roses, gladioli blossoms, and lilies of the valley.

The two bridesmaids, and matron of honor, Misses Juanita and Jewel McBrown, Miss Elizabeth Kennedy and Mrs. Floy Blakeley Price, were attired alike in smart organdy frocks made on bouffant lines. Each wore hats of stiffened organdy, in color matching their frocks, designed with off the face brims of Queen Ann fashion. Each bridesmaid carried bouquets of roses. The maid of honor carried a bouquet of rose and gladioli blossoms, and the matron of honor carried a bouquet of roses and yellow Peruvian lilies.

Preceding the bridesmaids, maid and matron of honor to the altar were Mr. George N. Redd of New York City, Mr. Glass' best man, and Dr. C. M. Steward and Mr. L. Kennedy, ushers. Following the bridesmaids, and matron of honor, came the ring bearer, Master Adolphus Donegan and the tiny flower girl, little Miss Laura Jean, who scattered roses in the path of the bride.

The bride's table, arranged in the dining room, was

The wedding party.

centered by the three tiered wedding cake, topped with a miniature bride and groom, and embossed with white roses and lilies of the valley. White tapers in silver and crystal candelabra lighted the table.

Immediately after the ceremony the bride and groom left for a trip to Niagara Falls, Philadelphia, Cleveland and other eastern points. They will make their home at Texas College, Tyler, Texas, where Mr. Glass has been president for the past five years.

President Glass wanted only the best for his bride, and soon he whisked her away to a honeymoon in Niagara Falls. They traveled by Pullman car, making the long trip from Texas to Canada. After their stay at the Falls, they traveled home via Ohio, where his family entertained the new bride.

The couple returned to Tyler and settled into their lives as leaders of the college, but the romance was not over. In fact, Mr. Glass was so pleased with his bride that he soon replaced the first ring with a magnificent new diamond ring—a major stone surrounded by rows and rows of smaller ones that together dazzled the eye of the most sophisticated observer.

At my daughter's wedding we will invite paupers and millionaires; white, Hispanic, and black; important and unknowns; no friend or acquaintance will be left out.—E. J. Campbell

Chapter 6

A New Career

Teach me thy way, O Lord, and I will walk in thy truth.
Psalms 86:11

Founded in 1894 by a group of ministers of the Christian Methodist Episcopal Church, Texas College is a four-year historically black institution of higher education. The campus of twenty-five acres is located in Tyler, Texas, where lakes and woodlands and shady, dogwood-lined streets abound. The academic focus is on humanities and education, business and social science, and natural sciences, computer science, and mathematics. President D. R. Glass presided over the programs with strong leadership and high standards, and as a result, Texas College became known as a place that produced fine teachers with strong programs in science and social science. Many of Dr. Glass' students went on to become successful in fields of business, law, medicine, and education.

Today the college has as its mission a program of educational study that contributes to the intellectual, social, physical, emotional, and spiritual development of each student. The college offers programs in arts and sciences, special programs, and in education. Texas College has an open admissions policy to serve a broad-based, traditional and non-traditional student clientele who are predominantly African-American. Many of the students are first-generation college students.

When the Glasses married, Texas College was one of only two Texas institutions of higher education that welcomed African-American students.

THE PRESIDENT'S WIFE

As soon as the honeymoon was over and President and Mrs. Glass were back home in Tyler, Willie Lee's real career began. It seemed that all her schooling and all her experiences had prepared her for this task. She determined to be the best possible president's wife. And with President Glass' guidance, she set a threefold goal for herself as the president's wife. She would work with individual students to enrich their college years; she would lead the college's fund-raising efforts, and she would establish a home economics program for the college. (One of her long-term acquaintances said of her on her eighty-seventh birthday, "She has continued to work toward those goals to this day!")

She began at once to have groups of students to the President's Home. Football players came for dinner and learned about finger bowls, salad forks, and best table manners. They learned not only through the experience of dining, but also how to handle social situations correctly. Female students were invited for teas and talked about how to present themselves in the most professional way. When Willie Lee's knowledge of home economics was paired with President Glass' conservative moral code, the students learned a great deal about how to conduct themselves as Texas College students.

Willie Lee knew the importance of the arts, and she wanted the Texas College students to be exposed to the best the nation had to offer. With President Glass' approval, she set out to bring nationally known artists to the campus. By allying herself and Texas College with the Tyler Chamber of Commerce, she brought famous performers to the campus: Marian Anderson, Roland Hayes, Graham Jackson, and Walter White, to name a few.

The president's own moral code greatly influenced rules for students in the days before World War II. For example, all female students were required to wear hose to classes, and, of course, no form of trousers were allowed at any time for the girls. Male students were required to attend classes in shirts and ties. Social events were carefully monitored. If there was a dance, it was a very restricted form of dancing. With the college band providing the music, couples danced without touching. The girl danced in front of the man, who followed her using the same steps. It was only later, after the changes brought about by the great war, that round dancing was allowed.

Soon after she arrived at Texas College, Willie Lee began lobbying for a home economics program for the college. President Glass took great pride in her interest and her knowledge of the subject, and with his support and leadership, the program was soon instituted.

Mrs. Glass taught the first classes in her home. Students who enrolled for foods and nutrition classes sat around the dining table for lectures, then had their labs in the Glasses' own kitchen.

For clothing classes, garments were cut out on the dining table and sewn on Mrs. Glass' sewing machine that was set up on the sunporch. For quantity foods, students used the school cafeteria kitchen. Other classes met in equally resourceful environments. Of course Mrs. Glass' intention from the beginning was to have a home economics building, and she soon began fundraising efforts to get the building.

One of her former students was asked about Mrs. Glass' teaching:

> The first class I had from Mrs. Glass was called "Social Fundamentals." I remember we sat in rows in front of her desk, and she began with instructions on how we were to behave and on how we were to prepare each

Students

of the class assignments. She had detailed instructions. For example, she told us we were only to come to her class if we were clean and well-groomed. She told us to be careful about putting too much oil on our hair. We were to wear hose to class each day, and of course, we were to wear only dresses—no one ever thought of wearing pants anywhere in those days.

When we turned in our class assignments, the papers were to be folded in a certain way; our names must appear in the upper right hand corner, and we were to use only black ink. I remember that she scared me almost to death on that first class day.

After those instructions, we had to write a short paper, then fold it and deliver it to her desk. Each girl carried her paper up to the desk with Mrs. Glass standing tall and straight watching each delivery. As I laid my paper on the desk, she said, "Wait just a minute."

I thought, *Oh, Lord, I've already done something wrong!*

She said, "Your paper looks very nice." With a sigh of relief I moved on.

But soon I learned she was a lady who deserved our respect and admiration. She had high standards, and she demanded a lot from us, but she was full of praise for each of us. She would say, "you can do that" or "well-done" or "you are the person we need for this job." She kept us working, working, all the time, but she soon became my idol.

We thought her house and everything she did was perfect. I wanted to be just like her. That first year, after I took her housing course, I went home for Christmas and tried to modernize everything in my family's home. I remember sawing apart a fine piece of furniture to make it look "modern." I repainted everything I could in my mother's house. Mrs. Glass just had that kind of influence on all her students.

She was our idol.

Mrs. Glass taught home economics at Texas College from 1939 to 1950. And during that time a fine new modern building was erected on the campus for the home economics program. It was appropriately named the "Willie Lee Campbell Glass Building."

FUNDRAISING

Mrs. Glass knew how to raise money. Her fundraising efforts began with concession stands at every athletic event. Hot dogs, hamburgers, tuna sandwiches, candy, homemade ice cream, lemonade, popcorn, popcorn balls—the

Willie Lee Glass Home Economics Building, Texas College, Tyler, Texas.

list was endless. If Mrs. Glass and the girls thought students would buy it, they cooked it and displayed it attractively in the concession stands. Seldom did games end with anything left to sell.

Willie Lee Campbell Glass had not watched her parents' resourcefulness without learning much from them, and she knew that there were many other ways besides selling food in concession stands to get money for her school. Soon she had had the girls in her classes long enough to have them well trained in all the skills valued in the best homes in Tyler. By carefully selecting her first consumer, she made it known that a crew of home economics students from Texas College was available to work in local homes. They could work with the homemaker to plan, prepare, serve, and host dinners, coffees, teas, and receptions. Before long they were in demand all over town, and the fund for the building began to grow.

With her at the president's side, the Tyler community began to take more notice of Texas College. Soon the new Mrs. Glass began receiving invitations to speak at events ranging from Sunday school to women's organizations. In each presentation she found a way to present the opportunities for people to share in the work of Texas College. The fund grew even larger.

She became acquainted with elected officials in Tyler, with bankers, ministers—in fact, with all the people who could help make Texas College a place of excellence. Her life became a constant round of entertaining potential givers and making presentations to individuals and groups who could help Texas College. She became a strong advocate not only for Texas College but also for all church-related colleges.

She was an excellent speaker, but she was at her best working one-on-one with people whom she could influence to join the cause of education for young people. An admirer said, "She had learned from her parents to adjust to whatever situation presented itself, and she learned from them how to handle people. She knows who to call for just what is needed. And people admire and respect her so much, and they know her causes are so worthwhile, that they always respond."

LEADERSHIP

People who are interviewed about Mrs. Glass provide interesting insights to her character, her philosophy, and her leadership. One woman who has worked closely with her since she was a student at Texas College had this to say about Mrs. Glass:

"Mrs. Glass was First Lady at Texas College because she was first and foremost the help mate of the president. He respected her ideas and her wishes, and he gave her freedom to carry out the projects she chose to lead for the good of the College. I have always admired her a great deal. Even as a student, I was captivated by her.

"When I was attending Texas College, my father would visit the campus often, and he usually saw Mrs. Glass during his visits. She always greeted him with genuine pleasure and she would tell him how well I was doing. She expressed her pride in my work. These comments, of course, made him feel good. One day as I was riding home with him for the weekend, he mused about our conversations with Mrs. Glass, and he turned to me and asked, 'Is she just putting on or is she sincere?' I said, 'Oh, she is sincere; that's her way.' My dad replied, 'Well, she must be sincere, because if she is putting on she would be tired by now!'

"A year or so later when I knew her well enough to repeat the comments to her, Mrs. Glass beamed with satisfaction, saying, 'Why that's one of the greatest compliments I ever received. You know, I like your papa.'

"Of course, my conversations at home on weekends were filled with my activities at Texas College. One evening as we sat by the fireside and the family listened and listened to me talk, my mischievous little brother interrupted me and asked, 'Is there anybody at that college beside this Mrs. Glass?'

"It is a strange phenomenon for one lady to accomplish so much. She has always had the ability to envision projects, set goals, and involve whomever it took to reach the goals. She helped define tasks, set parameters, develop strategies, and assess resources to reach goals for Texas College.

"Her ability to involve others weighed heavily in her accomplishments. Hard work was expected of every individual she involved.

"In the years when her husband was the president of the college, she probably did 90% of the recruitment. She would find bright young people in the high schools and convince them to come to Texas College. Many have made significant contributions to society because she helped them to see and develop their own potential.

"She was the invisible superintendent of buildings and grounds, purchasing agent, dietitian, general troubleshooter for the college, and even so, she had time to be an excellent teacher!"

Another person who was interviewed for this biography spoke of Mrs. Glass' unusual ability to persuade people to become involved with worthwhile endeavors. "She is a lady with a thousand strings!" he said. "If something is to be done, Mrs. Glass knows who to get to do it."

An editor of one of the Tyler newspapers spoke of her as the "unstoppable" Willie Lee Glass. "Even a freight train can't stop her," he reported after she survived a near fatal car-train collision.

"You'll never be able to walk again," the doctor told her after the accident. But the "unstoppable" Willie Lee was walking quite well just a few months later.

TO THE STATE OFFICE

By 1950, far-sighted educators could see that integration of the public schools was inevitable—it was simply a matter of time. In Texas, integration occurred as late as 1967 in some schools, but the Supreme Court ruling on integration was only five years away when the Texas commissioner of education offered Mrs. Glass a position with the Texas Education Agency in 1950.

At that time, vocational education was a powerful component of the education organization in Texas, and agriculture and home economics were the most prominent of the vocational programs. In 1950, the state agency already had three black consultants, but none of them were in home economics. The commissioner of education, Dr. Edgar, asked Ruth Huey, head of home economics in Texas, to find a black woman who could become a respected consultant for the entire state. As Ms. Huey pondered the challenge of finding just the right person, the name Willie Lee Campbell Glass was suggested to her over and over. Daughter of successful teachers and educational leaders, an attractive, mature woman who related well to everyone, an educator with high standards, a teacher with years of proven successes, the wife of a college president, an accomplished fundraiser, a public speaker in demand. But how could Ms. Huey persuade her to share her role as the college president's wife with the state of Texas?

After careful strategic planning, Ms. Huey called to her office J. C. McAdams, the most prominent of the black agriculture consultants.

"Mr. McAdams," she said, "we need your help badly. Texas absolutely must have a black home economics consultant on the Texas Education Agency staff. My staff and I have evaluated every black home economist in the state and there is no doubt that Willie Lee Glass is the best person for the job. But persuading her to come will be almost impossible. We have decided that you are the one to influence the Glasses for her to take the job."

"But Ms. Huey," he responded, "what woman would take it? She wouldn't be able to even enter a hotel where you have your meetings—much less have a room in any hotel in the state. She can't eat in a restaurant where your people meet. She will be ridiculed at most of the white schools she visits. It's hopeless."

"Mr. McAdams," Ms. Huey responded, "we can overcome all those barriers if we can get Mrs. Glass, and the commissioner and I expect you to help us hire her; in fact, Mr. McAdams, your success in this task may influence your job as well."

McAdams left the office shaking his head. But the next day, he went back to Huey's office and said, "I'll talk to Mrs. Glass after you and the commissioner make the offer."

True to his word, when he was told the time was right he drove to Tyler to meet with the Glasses. He had decided on just the right approach.

"Mrs. Glass," he said, "you just have to take this position. You must do it for the people of Texas, not just for our people, but for the future of public education in Texas. You can make a difference in how the events that are bound to occur in the next few years are played out."

"You have been to an integrated school," he continued, "and you are the only one we have to begin to break the barriers."

The Glasses listened to Mr. McAdams and finally agreed to consider the offer.

They pondered how their lives might change and how they might work with Willie Lee in Tyler and in Austin, and in fact, all over the state. At last, they decided she would take the job for one year. That year expanded to a time of service from 1950 to 1977 as a consultant for the Texas Education Agency.

"Mrs. Glass, how did you manage the travel?" asked an interviewer.

"Oh, the travel was no problem. Sometimes I flew from city to city and rented a car to drive to the various schools. Sometimes I had a car and driver, and occasionally another home economics teacher would drive me. The problems were not associated with travel; rather they were with hotels and restaurants. Often I had to stay overnight in a town, and when I did the only option for me was to stay in private homes. Actually, I have stayed in lovely, lovely homes with the nicest people. Home economics teachers, school superintendents, ministers of black churches, former students, family friends, Ms. Huey's friends—all these people took me in. Their guest rooms were clean and comfortable, often adorned with fresh flowers and every convenience.

"Since I couldn't get service in a restaurant, I was often allowed to go in the back door of a hotel, go quietly up to another white consultant's room and have food brought there for my meals. The other consultants looked out for me; they always found a way for me to have a place to sleep and good food."

A former home economics student was interviewed with questions about events of the fifties.

"I remember my home economics teacher (white) talking to my mother after we returned from a state meeting of the home economics youth organization. She told my mother that the State had hired a Negro woman as a consultant, and the woman attended the meeting. My teacher said that when the consultants and teachers went to a restaurant after the meeting they were told they could not come in if they tried to bring the Negro woman. She said the whole group turned and left. Eventually, they gave up on finding a restaurant that would serve them, and they bought food and took it to their rooms to eat. They secretly took the Negro lady into their room when no one was watching. My mother said, 'that's not right.' I remember pondering that conversation as I grew up with the trauma of integration at school."

Mrs. Glass' role at TEA was to visit school superintendents all across the state advising them on the needs of all students, including those in the black schools. Early on, she developed a strategy for achieving acceptance, and not once did she experience the negative reception that Mr. McAdams had predicted for her.

This is what she did as a matter of practice. First, she and Ms. Huey decided on an itinerary for her for a period of time, and then they charted each school to be visited. Mrs. Glass immediately began to research not only the school district, but the school superintendent as well. By the time she arrived at the school she knew the strengths of the superintendent, the principal of the colored high school, and the local home economics teachers.

With that information she could approach each person in a positive manner.

She said she had very few problems in all her twenty-four years of working with the schools of the state. Once, when integration was on the horizon, she visited a school superintendent who was in the process of building a new home economics department for the white high school. After complimenting him on the fine new building, Mrs. Glass told him he needed to add at least two sewing machines to the laboratory in the black school in order to meet state minimum standards. The man told her he had no money to do that, and even with tactful reasoning on Mrs. Glass' part, he steadfastly refused to buy anything for the school.

Mrs. Glass left the school worried about how to handle the matter. Home again in Tyler, she discussed it with Mr. Glass. "You may as well leave it alone," he advised. "Those white folks will never go against each other."

"We will see," replied Willie Lee, and in her report to the state office she noted the refusal of the district to meet state standards.

In a few weeks, Dr. Edgar, the state commissioner of education, notified the offending school district that their permit to offer vocational courses would be revoked if they could not buy the necessary equipment for all their laboratories. Soon the black school had the necessary sewing machines.

Mr. Glass laughed and said, "Willie Lee, you are something else. I never thought that would happen!"

Mrs. Glass had long been a fan of Dr. Edgar's. Perhaps he won her admiration early on in her tenure with the state. At that time there was to be a banquet for all teachers at a large state function, and Mrs. Glass and the other Negro TEA staff were told that they could come but that there would be a separate table for them. A few days passed, and Mrs. Glass went into Ms. Huey's office and said, "Ms. Huey, we think we just won't be able to come to the banquet, but thank you for inviting us." Later in the week, Dr. Edgar put out this memo, "Never again will my staff be discriminated against; they will all be treated equally!" There was no more separate seating.

In the fifties it was the custom of the national home economics organization to sponsor an annual meeting of all the student organizations. Called the Future Homemakers of America (FHA) they represented a large segment of America's youth. At the same time, students in the Colored High Schools had an organization called Negro Homemakers of America (NHA). In 1953 the national meeting of the FHA was scheduled for Salt Lake City, Utah. It was to be a big event, and Edna Amidon, national head of home economics, said that the NHA must be invited to participate in the national conference. School superintendents in Texas said that couldn't be done. It just wouldn't do to try to have the whites and Negroes together. Leaders at TEA argued the issue for days. Finally, one of them said that it might work if they were able to get Willie Lee Glass to lead the black delegation. And so it was that the national meeting occurred with both black and white students present.

The black girls were a success, for under Willie Lee's guidance they knew just how to behave and just what was expected of them. Before they left Texas, Mrs. Glass had put together a handbook for travelers, explaining what clothes were needed, how to pack, and how to behave in a hotel—elevators and checking-in, conferencing, and living in a hotel room—all new experiences. For many of the girls, the entire trip was a first. None of them had traveled out of state, and most had not been out of their own hometowns.

During the meeting, the white delegates pooled their money and bought a silver tray to present to Miss Amidon at one of the sessions. When the black girls saw that happen without their opportunity to participate, they immediately went to Mrs. Glass.

"Don't get angry," she advised, "just think, and plan your response."

Her response to the incident was to go at once to a local florist and order a corsage of red roses. She directed exactly how it was to be designed. The roses were to be interspersed with tightly rolled dollar bills. That evening, the black girls presented the corsage to Miss Amidon. The gracious lady put it on and wore it for the remainder of the conference.

"Now, you see," said Mrs. Glass to the girls, "it's better to act positively than defensively!"

When asked about the turbulent times of the sixties and seventies, Mrs. Glass says, "I was taught to always think positively, to practice nonviolence, and to respect all people. Papa said, 'Never, never, let yourself get into a fight.' That philosophy helped me get through that transition period of time in our country."

Papa said, "Don't ever leave a job after just one year—stay at least two so that the record will show you could have stayed longer if you wished to do so."—WLCG

Too noble for anger; too courageous for doubt; too full of God's love to hate.—WLCG

Chapter 7

A Time of Transition

Let the evil of the wicked come to an end, but establish thou the righteous, thou who triest the minds and hearts.
Psalms 7:9

The big, long, shiny black car pulled up to the Austin Building on the campus of Stephen F. Austin State College in Nacogdoches, and a well-groomed young black man came from behind the driver's seat to open the back door of the car. Out stepped a tall, beautiful woman. She was bronze-skinned, with perfectly coiffured coal-black hair. Her clothing had the classic, expensive look of a woman of means, and she carried herself with confidence as she climbed the steps to the front door of the college's administration building.

Two coeds in bobby socks and poodle skirts of the 1950s were crossing the campus at the time, and as they observed the arrival, one said, "Wasn't that a black woman going in the Austin Building? What could she be doing here?"

"And through the front door too," added her friend. "How strange!"

A few minutes later, the woman exited the building in the company of a white woman from one of the offices in the building. The chauffeur seated the ladies in the backseat of the big car, and the vehicle rolled out onto the highway, with the women looking the part of regal ladies transported by a smartly dressed driver. No one on the campus of the small East Texas college campus had seen anything like that in the life of the institution.

The ladies were Willie Lee Campbell Glass and Marie Healey, newly appointed consultants for the Texas Education Agency, and they were making their first visit as supervisors of home economics education in the state's high schools. It was the beginning of Mrs. Glass' twenty-four-year career with the state education agency. Her work as a consultant began in 1950 as the unrest among the races was peaking to the point of the Supreme Court decision of 1955 that made segregated schools illegal. And it continued through the stressful years of integration until she retired in 1974.

Mrs. Glass never talked about the years as the time of integration, but rather as "a time of transition."

That first visit took her and Mrs. Healey, her co-worker, to high schools in Newton County—those areas of Deep East Texas that give the area the image of remoteness and isolation. Many homes in the area lacked indoor plumbing, electricity, and other common comforts that the supervisors enjoyed in their own lives. Poverty and illiteracy were well known among the people in the beautiful pine forest.

Mrs. Healey, a young professional woman who had been reared in the plains of far West Texas, later described the first school they visited:

> It was a very small building, set way back in the woods, down a narrow dirt road. Tall, pine trees shaded the building, and under the pines were great clusters of dogwood trees. I had never seen those trees with their magnificent white blossoms. And on the creek bank that ran beside the school, wild azaleas bloomed, and there were masses of ferns growing all the way to the edge of the water trickling over sand and stone. I stood in awe of one of the prettiest sights I had ever seen, and though the resources for teaching that we found inside the little high school were woefully limited, I continued to be daz-

Colleagues and Friends

Above:
Ms. LaVerne Madlock, colleague and assistant.

Right:
Consultants

Bottom:
Consultants Healey, Smith, Glass, and Pitman.

zled by the beauty of the setting. As we left, I turned to the Negro Homemaking Teacher and said, "I know it is a joy to teach in a beautiful place like this."

The woman looked at me in a startled way, and without saying a word, turned and went back into the school. I guess she thought I was too naive to have any understanding of the demands of her work in that place. But after all these years I remember that first trip with Mrs. Glass as one of wonder and pleasure.

At another school we visited that day the homemaking students served a fine lunch to us, the school superintendent, and president of the local school board. I was unsure of how to discuss our concerns with these important men, but Mrs. Glass spoke to them with confidence about the needs of the schools. She pointed out the standards for equipping a homemaking laboratory and told the men that she was sure they would want her to be able to report to the State Department that their schools—both the black and the white schools—meet the standards. After some tactful, but clear discussion, the men decided they would put some additional equipment for the black high school in their next budget. Mrs. Glass complimented them on their decision, and we were soon on our way back to Nacogdoches.

On that two-hour drive, I got the first of many lessons in the different lifestyles that society forced on the races. It happened when we stopped for gas. I had always been accustomed to taking the opportunity of a gas stop for a restroom visit, but I noticed immediately that Mrs. Glass made no move to get out of the car. Wondering why, I suddenly realized that the service station restrooms were for "whites only." We simply disciplined ourselves to wait for a rest stop until we reached my home in Nacogdoches. That was the first of many times when I saw Mrs. Glass accept what she must, then rise above the unjust limitations.

Mrs. Healey continued to talk of their early days of working together. On their first trip to Austin for staff meeting, the commissioner of education asked the consultants from all the programs to divide themselves into small groups and sit together at tables to work on new state regulations. As the groups formed, Mrs. Glass found herself (the only black person in the room) alone at a table. No one was willing to sit with her. She said that in a very few minutes, Commissioner Hubert looked around the room and saw what was happening. "Oh, Mrs. Glass," he called out, "I want you to serve as my secretary." After that the others seemed to accept her; there was no more sitting at a table alone.

WORKING WITH THE SUPERINTENDENTS

The first years of her work with the state agency preceded integration, and in school after school Mrs. Glass found glaring inequities between the white and the black laboratories. The concept of "separate but equal" was far from reality. However, regardless of the situation she found, Mrs. Glass approached school leaders with a calm dignity that was almost always returned with respectful response. She seldom spoke of unequal treatment of the high schools. Rather, she talked of state standards and the need for them to be met in order for students to achieve at their optimum capacity. If a superintendent was reluctant, she would tactfully remind him that he ran the risk of state funding being withheld if the state standards were not met.

Mrs. Glass set high standards for herself and for her work. For example, she was always perfectly groomed and professionally dressed. She was a visual model of excellence as she traveled among the schools—whether she was in rural or urban areas, in black or white schools, visiting a single classroom or speaking at a national level conference—her personal demeanor and appearance was always perfection. Likewise, she approached every person with respect and tact.

Coworkers were amazed at the response she got from the white school superintendents. "Not all of them welcomed an African-American woman as a supervisor," one of them explained, "but she behaved with each of them like such a lady, and with such professionalism, that they usually came around."

As racial tensions increased during the 1950s, Mrs. Glass found herself frequently calling on her father's strategies to deal with difficult situations. For example, when she presented one superintendent with the need for more sewing machines for the homemaking department in the black school, he said, "I can't spend any money there this year; besides in a few years integration will come, and the equipment won't be needed. In the meantime, I have to use every available dollar for the new white high school I'm building."

"But, Mr. Jones," Willie Lee replied, "it is the group of girls in this year's program who need equipment for learning."

"I'm sorry," he said, "I can't do anything for them."

Willie Lee reported to Ms. Huey (the state head of home economics) and Ms. Huey said, "Fine, but we will have to withhold the funds for all his vocational programs." True to her words, the letter of withdrawal went out.

Soon a call came from the superintendent. "You'd pull my approved units from the white school?" he asked in disbelief.

"We have no other choice," replied Ms. Huey.

"Humph," came the response over the long-distance wire. "I'll rework my budget to meet your requirements."

When Willie Lee reported the story to Mr. Glass, he said, "It's a wonderful time; I never thought I'd see anything like that in my day!"

On another occasion, Mrs. Glass was to visit a town near Nacogdoches, and she heard by the grapevine that the school superintendent had instructed his teachers to go downtown and borrow from a local store some furniture and equipment to make the Negro homemaking department look well furnished. Sure enough, when she arrived the department had everything that was needed to meet state standards. But, as she had expected, the equipment all looked totally unused—brand new, in fact.

As was her practice, after touring the department and talking with some of the students and the teacher, Mrs. Glass stopped by the superintendent's office. As they talked, she said, "Mr. Smith, you people are so hospitable; I feel so comfortable here. Would you mind if I just popped in for another visit in a few weeks?"

"When would you want to come?"

"Oh, just some day when I am passing through town on my way to visit other schools and my mother in Nacogdoches."

"Who are your parents?"

"E. J. and Mary Campbell."

"Professor Campbell was your father? My, my, what a surprise. Well, sure, come anytime. And by the way, we'll be keeping all that new furniture and equipment we've been trying out."

Mrs. Glass used all sorts of strategies to get resources for the teaching laboratories. Many were those she had seen her father use. One of her former students described a strategy this way:

"When we opened the Tea Room at Texas College we could not afford air conditioning. Mrs. Glass used her father's strategies that had worked at E. J. Campbell High School. This is what she did: On a summer day when a group of wealthy white women had reserved the Tea Room, she borrowed twenty-four of the smallest electric fans she could find and she placed them all around the room. Set in strategic spots, the women could hardly move around without bumping into one of them. As they left the building, the women were heard to exclaim over and over about how delicious the meal was and about how beautifully the young women served. Then one said, "I'll tell you one thing, I'm going to see they get air conditioning in this place!" And so they did; the friends contributed money for the full cost of the system."

Professor's Campbell's methods had worked again!

WORKING WITH TEACHERS

One of Mrs. Glass' responsibilities was to provide in-service for teachers all across the state. She worked with them individually, in small groups, and at statewide conferences. She was an excellent presenter, in demand at state and national levels. Leaders in the state office said that anytime there was a choice of workshops, teachers always chose her sessions first. Only when hers were filled did other presenters get participants.

"Why was she so popular?" an interviewer asked a teacher from that time period.

> Because she had something to offer, and because she presented her workshops in such appealing ways. First, she was a handsome woman, well-groomed, and beautifully dressed. She greeted us as if she were interested in each one of us as individuals. In her presentations she used visual aids, roleplay, and audience participation. And she always sent us away with handouts to be used back home in our classes.
>
> She was extremely helpful as we approached integration. She helped us to understand the culture of these new students we were to have. In conference after conference she had us work in small groups to roleplay ways students might feel when they were thrust into the white schools. Then we teachers discussed various responsive strategies.
>
> She helped us understand children of poverty, different family values, and diverse lifestyles. I remember that once in a workshop she said to a homemaking teacher, "You have a fine lesson on proper ways to make a bed—how to miter the corners of the top sheet and the bottom sheet so that the two fit together neatly, but have you thought of how you will teach the lesson when you have students in your class whose family has no sheets?

She often talked of expectations for student achievement. "Your expectations for achievement must vary from student to student depending on the educational level the students bring to the class," she explained. Closely related to expectations for success was the need to examine instructional methods, realizing that the black children may never have been exposed to some learning experiences that were common in white schools. She explained an example: "If children have been accustomed to preparing reports by simply copying material verbatim from an encyclopedia, then reading it to the class when their time for presentation comes, they will be extremely frustrated when you expect the report to be a combination of ideas from many sources, reported orally with only an outline to guide the student speaker. You must accept the fact that there are differences. Learn what they are; then you have a chance of overcoming the problems caused by the differences," she believed.

"Those were prickly times" explained a teacher from Tyler. "One time just after we integrated, we went to the State FHA meeting, and Ms. Huey [the state director] learned that one of the people on the program was scheduled to sing the Stephen Foster song, 'Old Black Joe.' She was afraid the song might not be appropriate at this particular time.

" 'I know what we'll do,' she said. 'We'll have him sing it to Mrs. Glass and let her decide if it will be offensive to anyone in the audience.'

"So that's what they did; the young man met Mrs. Glass in the auditorium and sang the song for her.

" 'Oh, that's all right,' responded Mrs. Glass, 'it's a fine song,' and the show went on as planned."

Mrs. Glass believed that every teacher had something of worth to share with others. And because she held so strongly to that belief, she used lots of group work in the in-service conferences she conducted. Teachers would work in groups to find solutions to problems or to share strategies for teaching, then Mrs. Glass would collect all the ideas they produced. When the products were sorted, edited, and united in a single document, there was a fine resource for the use of individual teachers to have back at home in their own workplace. Mrs. Glass always followed through by returning their ideas to the teachers in a resource packet.

Once, Dr. WillaVawn Tinsley, dean of the College of Education at Texas Tech, joined her in her efforts to bring people together. Again the time was before integration, when the in-service conferences for black and white teachers were held separately. Willie Lee was looking for a way to have one conference with the teachers together, and with Dean Tinsley's help she was successful. Here's what they did. When an invitation came for Dean Tinsley to speak to the white homemaking teachers at a large city school, she immediately called Mrs. Glass, and they set their plan in motion. She said, "Willie Lee, schedule a conference for your black teachers on this same day and in this same town. Invite me to speak, and when you get your conference approved, I'll notify the superintendent that I simply cannot deliver the same address twice in one day. I must have all the teachers in one place at one time and do a single presentation."

That's what they did, and as a result the black and white teachers came together for the first integrated home economics teachers in-service conference.

Finding strategies to bring whites and blacks together without conflict was usually a challenge. For example, one year just before integration, Marian Anderson agreed to come to Tyler for a concert at Texas College. Mrs. Anderson said in her contract that the audience must be integrated. The event was underwritten by several prominent people, all of whom expressed their desire to attend the performance. Each was to be asked to sit on the stage. Some believed the seating should be integrated, while others insisted on segregated seating. As wife of the college president, Mrs. Glass was in charge of the seating arrangements. What a dilemma she faced! Finally, she created a plan to satisfy both camps. The sections of seats were arranged to give a pattern of integration not only for financial contributors but by race as well. There were several rows of chairs placed in front and on the sides of the stage; one row would be for blacks and the other would be for whites. In this way, they were both integrated, by being seated in the same section, and they would be separated, by being seated in separate rows. Advance design and sale of tickets coupled with trained ushers helped tremendously in getting attendees in assigned seats. Apparently the plan worked, for no one was heard to complain. With Mrs. Glass' planning and Ms. Anderson's singing, it was pronounced a perfect evening.

WORKING WITH STUDENTS

Mrs. Glass modeled good teaching. As she visited schools around the state, she actually taught classes for the teachers, and when she visited colleges and universities, she often taught home economics methods classes. Whether she was teaching young people or adults, she acted on two strongly held beliefs about teaching.

"First," she said, "a teacher must get the student involved. And if you can get the children, or even adult students, to feel good about themselves, to have a sense of belonging, they will be willing to participate." In short, secure the interest of students or those you teach—give a clear understanding and provide opportunities for subsequent use of the skill taught.

With a class of children she did not know, Mrs. Glass would often begin by saying to the children, "Let's play a game called 'What's in a Name?'" Then she would demonstrate a process of describing her positive attributes by naming a personality characteristic that was spelled with a letter in her name. For example, she might say, "My name is Willie. W is for willing to work; I is for intelligent; L is for loving; L is also for lovely; I is for interested in the world around me; and E is for energetic. Could I be willing to work, intelligent, loving, lovely, interested in nature, and energetic? Yes, I could be, and you too can describe yourself with your name. Your name is special. Your mother and father gave it to you; its yours alone. Let's spell your first name and find a characteristic that each letter represents.

Who will begin? Here is Meg; let's start with her: M is for mature; E is for eager to learn; and G is for a good person. Is Meg a mature, eager to learn student, and a good person? I believe she is. Now each of you try your name."

Mrs. Glass remembers that once long ago after she spent time with a class using the name game she left the class to visit the principal. As she walked down the hall, a little boy came running down the hall calling to her. "Lady," he called, "come here; you didn't ask my name," and tears welled up in his eyes. She turned and, going back to where he stood, hugged him to her and said, "I thought I did; let's do it now. Tell me again who you are."

"Sam."

"Oh," she said, "then we can say 'S is for smart; A is for active; and M is for the man you are becoming. You are a smart, active man! I'm so glad I met you, Sam."

Mrs. Glass used music to create another technique to help students feel accepted. She selected taped music that represented each culture in the school, and had it playing in the background as students entered the classroom. She explained to methods students that hearing their own type of music in the class creates a sense of belonging among students. This was particularly important as integration began.

Second, Mrs. Glass believed in high standards. This was evident in her work at Texas College. She taught the young black women to be well-groomed, to select hair styles that were not too oily, to dress appropriately, and to use good manners wherever they were. She insisted that they learn all the rules and principles that guided their work—in nutrition, food service, entertaining, home management, or child care. She would say to her perspective young teachers, "If you look and act like a person of reason, people will believe you have something to teach them that is worthwhile."

Mrs. Glass believed in lessons that included application of knowledge. She presented the knowledge base, then she planned ways in which students would immediately apply it. "The sooner the knowledge is applied, the more learning takes place," she emphasized to methods students. If laboratories were not appropriate for the subject she was teaching, she made liberal use of visual aids, role play, case studies, and other types of student involvement. In addition, she provided as many field experiences as possible for students. For example, foods and nutrition students at Texas College also operated a Tea Room that was established for both a learning labortory and a fundraiser at the college.

Youth organizations were a special interest and responsibility of Mrs. Glass during her years with the Texas Education Agency. In vocational home economics, students learned leadership skills through participation in a youth organization. During integration, the organizations were called, for white students, Future Homemakers of America (FHA), and for black students, New Homemakers of America (NHA). With integration on the horizon, Mrs. Glass was charged with preparing the NHA girls to join the FHA, and with providing experiences for the two groups to share. Mrs. Glass' work was augmented by the work of two additional black supervisors: Mrs. Ruth Payne Smith and Mrs. Hattie Marie Baker, who were supervisors of Areas II and III, respectively. Early on in Ruth Payne Smith's tenure, her responsibility led her to become the state NHA advisor. Later, Mrs. Mable Tucker joined the team.

The ladies took their responsibilities with the youth organizations seriously. They made the Texas NHA organization as strong as possible. Members were required to memorize their creed, learn the objectives, attend meetings regularly, learn parliamentary procedure, and work for the organization. When they were to be on the program or attend a regional meeting, a great deal of time was spent practicing and role playing their responsibilities. Each traveling member learned how to enter a hotel lobby, how to greet strangers, and how to talk with adult sponsors from other areas.

Mrs. Glass provided in-service education for black

home economics teachers in Texas on ways to prepare the black students to become members of FHA. Her goal was for the black students to be active and able members of the organization. She worked with both the state and national governing boards to make the integration of the organizations as smooth as possible.

"The three black supervisors felt they failed in their attempt to get an integration of the NHA creed and objectives," she often reflected. "We lost those parts of the organization that were unique to NHA; we should have tried some different strategies."

Even though Mrs. Glass worked with students during the most troubled, tense times preceding integration, she never condoned violence in any form. For example, here is a story reported by a woman who was one of her Texas College students when sit-ins were a common practice.

The Texas College students had decided to stage a sit-in at the local Woolworth store, and unknown to any of the professors, the students organized and began their march from the campus. On the way, they encountered Mrs. Glass. She stopped them and engaged them in conversation. They were evasive about their intent, and finally she said, "You're going for a sit-in, aren't you?" When they admitted they were, she began this lecture: "We are all important people. This country is great because there are differences among us; just as a great pianist must use both white and black keys to produce great music, society needs black and white people. Our mission is to learn to work together to produce greatness. . . ." and so the lecture went.

The woman said that by the time Mrs. Glass finished, all the students were in tears with the emotion of her ideas, and they all went back to their dorm rooms. The woman said they did in fact march to a sit-in on another day, but they never forgot Mrs. Glass' philosophy about ways to relate to each other. Today, the woman who related that story chairs an academic department in a major university in Texas. She credits much of her success to Texas College and the Glass philosophy and training.

CHAPTER 8

Glass Reflections

Let the words of my mouth and the meditations of my heart be acceptable in thy sight, O Lord, my strength and my redeemer.

Psalms 19:14

Mrs. Glass' professional life placed her in three major roles: teacher, fundraiser, and educational consultant. In each of those roles, effective public speaking was required, and she was a master at the podium. To review her professional files is to see how carefully she prepared for each role, especially each speaking role. For these opportunities she spent hours in preparation; in fact she never took on any project without careful preparation.

To review the presentations she made as in-service training for teachers is to see how forward thinking she was when she was most active in training teachers during the '50s, '60s, and '70s. For example, today as educational leaders across the nation prepare for schools of the twenty-first century, their language is sprinkled liberally with such phrases as "collaboration," "clinical (or field) experiences," "hands-on class activities," "diversity," "learner-centered instruction" and "performance assessment." Readers will readily see that these are the very strategies Mrs. Glass proposed three decades ago.

The following pages in this chapter are filled with excerpts from her speeches and teacher workshops. Current pedagogy is found throughout the presentations.

From "There are Many Roads to Rome"

By the nature of our society we are committed to freedom, individualism, and rationality. Education is not a conducted tour through courses, credits, and examinations, but rather it is a total process of change in individual person. The challenge of teaching is one of applying relevance to the process.

From "Successful Teaching as a Matter of Relevance"

If teaching is to be relevant, if it is to be a positive force in educational improvement, it must prepare teachers to live and teach in a multi-cultural, multi-racial, multi-class world. To develop (within new teachers) ideas, propositions, generalizations, and theories that really relate to teacher and student behaviors, to the school, the classroom and the counseling session, the lessons must be delivered in a real teaching-learning environment, i.e., the real situation must be the primary laboratory. The road of relevance can be constructed by infusing professional education with the idea that the sciences, the humanities, and the arts are the means through which we come to grips with the nature of our own lives and of the world in which we live.

People who have achieved success in their careers are people who have trained and worked hard. Marian Anderson's voice has been described as a voice the likes of which will appear only every thousand years, but she practiced hours and hours for years to develop her talent. Joe Louis was not in the ring for the first time when he became heavyweight champion of the world. He trained and cultivated his talents until he was as good as God intended him to be. Ralph Bunche did not become one of the greatest peacemakers the world has ever known by playing truant from school; he studied for years, training the talent that was his.

From "Discovering Teachers' Special Abilities"

Successful, effective teachers are those who think clearly, are curious about ideas and things, have a broad range of interests and passions, see the relationships among ideas in several fields, behave, as well as talk, intelligently, and apply knowledge and reason to problems.

. . . Teachers must be prepared to teach and live in a multi-cultural, multi-racial, multi-class world. Perhaps some are weary of hearing about the disadvantaged child, the Civil Rights movement, and the problems of big city schools. They are weary because the language used to talk about these problems has become hackneyed, not because the problems have been solved. Teachers are called on to ponder these questions:

1. How can we get in touch with the realities of disadvantaged communities and school systems and with the needs of students who may compose the classes in those system?

2. How much feedback is there among student teachers, new teachers, and university professors who train them?

3. Is there direct contact between the experiences of the professors and the disadvantaged community to ensure that the concepts and strategies presented in the university classroom are applicable to the disadvantaged community?

4. How are we (as individuals) adapting to the changes brought about by transitions in our society?

5. Are there model schools where prospective teachers can gain direct field experience in a wide variety of cultural and other diverse characteristics?

From "Challenges of Teaching in the Inner City"

Teaching in the inner-city means "taking learning to the people." That is nothing new, but we must adapt the teaching-learning process to bring about involvement of whoever is present in our classes "today" with meaningful experiences.

How can teachers be prepared for working in our

inner cities? They must be taught in pre-service and in in-service with information gained through field experience, analysis, and research.

The teacher who will work in an inner city must understand the source of irritations, rebellion, and issues. Conflict that rebounds and strikes the persons who might be considered the urban poor simultaneously hits the classroom when the teacher is attempting to produce constructive learning. The teachers need realistic awareness of the social issues, the social sciences, the way people respond to tension, insecurity, distrust, and despair. These teachers must have these three vital abilities:

1. The ability to work as team members.
2. The ability to develop effective ways of guiding, directing, encouraging, and working with youth and adults.
3. The ability to understand the realism of the family life of the students.

Teachers must be change agents, focusing on families where they really are, and they must be visionaries to project an image of what may influence their well-being in the future.

From "Learner-centered Teaching"

If a teacher really believes in learner-centered teaching, he or she believes in these principles:

1. If a student is involved in choosing the techniques, he will be more accepting of the resulting situation.
2. If the learning situation is a part of real life or seems real to the student, she will perceive the relevance and be more eager to learn.
3. If a student is participating, mentally as well as physically, his interest will be greater and achievement more rapid.
4. If a student has personal interest in the success of the technique, motivation and learning are increased.
5. If the chosen techniques help a student to experience success, her self-esteem and motivation will be enhanced.

6. If a student finds pleasure in the learning situation, he is more likely to continue learning.

7. If a student develops skills for independent learning, she can continue to learn after formal school is finished.

8. If a student sees usefulness in learning activities, motivation will be increased.

9. If a student develops positive attitudes toward learning, she will be more likely to be content learning independently.

To be effective, the approaches to problems in the classroom must be varied just as much as the approaches to problems in the world of business and industry must vary. There is no one approach that is effective with all students. Varying styles of teaching are required to reach today's youth.

The teaching-learning situation must be relevant. Teachers committed to realism in curriculum development and program planning are teachers who will be successful.

Teachers are obligated to begin instruction for each child on the educational level where the child is. We are effective only so far as we are in touch with the realities of the children we have.

If we are to be effective as teachers we must:

- adapt ourselves to the changes into which the winds of transition (integration) have blown us
- act, react, and interact to the population of the inner cities and be cognizant of their values, goals, insecurities, aspirations, and hopes
- consider the dire need for pre-employment programs for youth
- educate our children to be the effective consumers they will become
- provide practical field experiences in as wide a variety of cultural areas as possible
- learn to be more observant, to interpret, to communicate more effectively, and to become constructive and visible change agents

- require students to assume greater responsibility for his own learning through inquiry, organization of facts and ideas, and through application of information from real life!

From "Kaleidoscope of Cultures—R. S. V. P."

[From a section of the speech that described the protected child of the privileged.] These are unfortunate children with a proverbial fence between themselves and others that makes them unknowledgeable of human differences. This lack of information affects their potential for life adjustment. Their status affects the learning process. For example, the story is told about a little girl in a wealthy private school who was asked to write a composition about a poor family. The child began the essay with these words: "This family was very poor. The mom was poor; the daddy was poor; the brothers and sisters were poor; the cook was poor; the chauffeur was poor; and the doorman was poor."

This composition is one of the most nearly perfect examples of innocence that I have ever seen. Innocence is beautiful! However, there is a great dependency involved in innocence. These children know less than any other about the world around them. They have had experiences in many beauty spots of the world. Yet they are deprived of the fullness of America's great culture. These children need knowledge and experiences that will remove the fence that shields them from the realities of life.

From "Important 'Ps' for Success"

- A Purpose for living
- A Positive outlook on life
- Participation in something constructive
- Pride in one's self
- Pride in one's culture
- Peace that reflects inner calm
- Absence of Prejudice that is the cancer of the soul that when left unchecked will destroy the soul by overpowering the heart and mind.

From "The Case of D Us"

The characteristics of a person who will bring about change:

1. She must be a motivator (cause something to happen).
2. She must be an instigator (start something).
3. She must be an educator (be knowledgeable of changing times).
4. She must be a communicator (listens and talks with people on their level of understanding).
5. She must be an evaluator (constantly checks to see "how are we doing?").

From "The Magic Number"

[A presentation to high school graduating seniors]

As you go from this place today, give thought to your next forty years—to your career. In planning for those forty years, I suggest four rules to serve as guides:

1. Live with a purpose.
2. Discover your own unique talents.
3. Work to develop your talents.
4. Use your talents in service.

. . . No one reaches the top of the ladder of success who has not, figuratively speaking, toiled in the night while his companions slept. I remind you of the race between the hare and the tortoise. Although the hare had more skill and speed, the race was won by the tortoise, for he moved while his companion slept.

. . . . A man will remain a rag-picker as long as he has only the vision of a rag-picker. It is a good plan to make a point to tackle one hard job every day. If we do this, we will find that we have exercised our willpower, our minds, and our bodies to good purpose.

We are expected to develop our talents so that we may serve all humankind. Talents are not to be buried in the sand; they are not to be used for selfish purposes. Talents are to be used for service. The person who does not strive to leave the world a better place than he found it, has seriously abused his talents.

And now, my dear graduates, blessed are you for "blessed is the man with new worlds to conquer." Go and conquer!

From "Church Related Colleges"
[A fundraising speech]

Scriptural foundation: Isaiah 54:1. *"Enlarge the place of thy tent, and let them stretch forth the curtains of thine habitations; spare not, lengthen thy cords, and strengthen they stakes."*

The church-related college has come into being because the church is concerned about Christian education. There is education and education, but only the church-related college gives Christian education. This is our saving power—it would be a sin to let that go—we would be letting down God's kingdom.

It is vital for college supporters to have an understanding of church college needs. Supporters must be in the know. For when people know, they care, and when they care, they share.

I am reminded of the homemaker and a plumber whom she called to fix a water problem in her kitchen. The charge was more than the homemaker expected, and when she asked for an analysis of the charges, the plumber said, "Ma'am, I charged $5 for the work that was needed to fix the problem, and $25 for knowing how to find the problem." Likewise we must be knowledgeable about the needs of our college.

Every time we feel that all has been done that needs to be done—that there is nothing further to be done—the charge comes clear and simple . . . SPARE NOT, LENGTHEN THY CORDS! The charge is to do more, on a bigger and wider scale—right in the place where you are.

The church-related college has three major needs: money and students and responsive alumni. Every business organization needs money, and the college is in the business of preparing people to serve. Therefore, we, the church-related college, need money.

The church-related college finds itself in competition with institutions receiving expanding support from public funds. This situation requires more than individual denominational effort. It requires an expanding cooperative spirit in area educational organizations. For example, Texas College may well develop a relation with the Interdenominational Theology Center, with the Colleges in Atlanta: Georgia Clark Spellman, Moorehouse, and others.

Gifts of money will only come to the college with a culture of cooperation, with good public relations, with a clear understanding of what we are about, with interest from faithful supporters, and with assistance from appropriate government agencies.

More important than money are the students who come to Texas College. We must search out capable and promising young men and women for our students. Send them to us. In slum areas of our large cities, the rate of unemployment is high—higher among youth than among any age group. Similarly, juvenile delinquency is high among high school dropouts. There is urgent need for action to stimulate the interest of our youth to secure higher education, preparing for the opportunities that will be available to the prepared. Determine in your community to have a program that will keep youth in high school. Sponsor organizations that build sound values into your youth. All this, we ask you to do so that you may send your young people to us. Those you send to us must be lovingly received back into the service of your community after they have completed their period of education with us.

The church-related school is a service agency, but in order to serve you, we must be served by you. We are grateful to you for the outpouring of love, gifts, and services you have given to us.

The church-related college has two major challenges: (1) how to maintain educational integrity and (2) how to exemplify Christian ethics.

Christian people believe in service. Someone has said the only difference between Heaven and Hell is service. The little money students pay does not support a college. In order for the colleges to survive they must be first class. They must offer all the values of a dedicated Christian Community at the price which the people believe it is worth.

From "Appreciation to the Texas College Family" on the occasion of their testimonial dinner for President Glass

Bishop and Mrs. Doyle, President and Mrs. Potts, members of the Eighth Episcopal District of the Christian Methodist Episcopal Church, guests and friends:

Understanding the fact that this special occasion is for my husband, I share with him the gratitude and soul-stirring essence that comes from the many wonderful things you have said and done for him tonight and through the years. As a wife, and at his request, I accept the responsibility to thank you for him.

We want to say thank you in a most simple manner. We want the manner to be simple in order that there will be no doubting of our sincerity.

We have stopped long enough to become aware of our blessings, and from the depth of our souls we say thank you.

We realize that gratitude is one of the noblest emotions of the human heart. It blesses those who give it worthy expression. It blesses those who are fortunate enough to receive it. It has brought sunshine into the darkest days and awakened songs in the night.

It is true that the guest of honor should be seen but not heard. But everybody knows that testimonial dinners are different. Here tonight we, the Glasses, want no personal glory, we are merely a symbol of something more important than personal glory—a greater Texas College. If the things you have done tonight are expressions of your love, esteem, and admiration for Mr. Glass, then I appeal to you to continue supporting the cause that rests heavily on his heart. He asks that we lift our eyes beyond today's horizons and resolve to conduct the affairs of Texas College so that Dr. and Mrs. Potts may write an even brighter chapter in our glorious history. The workers pass, but the work abides.

From our experience there are countless blessings God wants us to have, but some come with the price tag of suffering. Let us look upon suffering as the great blessing it is. We find those who suffer bravely learn how to bless and appreciate the work of others, which is perhaps the highest reward for living.

The attitude we take toward what happens is more important than what happens. We owe it to the Texas College Family to live in the bright side of life and to help each family member to realize how much God has done for us, and will do in every circumstance.

I am reminded now of Jesus' instruction to Peter when Peter professed his love for Jesus. Jesus said, "If you love me, feed my sheep." Mr. Glass is saying that if the things you have done tonight are an expression of your love, your admiration, or even your appreciation, then feed his sheep. Mr. Glass has been the shepherd of Texas College for 30 years and that shepherd is admonishing you tonight to continue to feed his sheep—Texas College.

The sheep, Texas College, must be fed in the coming years with your service to its purposes, with your adherence to its ideals, with your support of its philosophy, with your contribution to its physical progress, with your inspiration to its students and with your sacrifices to make it able to render the service fashioned by the dream of Mr. Glass.

Mr. Glass is aware that the progress and growth at Texas College has been the result of cooperation, understanding, and hard work for more than 67 years. This confidence is a source of support that will carry him to an island of inner contentment.

Of the many experiences that we have had in life together, none have been so arrayed as these tonight. And for these acts of kindness, we thank you and may the bright spirit "Feed my Sheep" make a singing melody in your hearts forever.

A story from one of her speeches:

On a cold winter day, a little boy with no shoes was walking the icy streets of Chicago. A kind lady took him by the hand and led him to a nearby store and asked the clerk to dry and warm his feet and put socks and shoes on him. "Please make all charges to me," she said. The little boy in amazement could not at first say a word, but as the lady started for the door, the little boy cried out, "Wait lady, are you Christ's wife?"

Service is the rent we pay for living in God's world.

Chapter 9

Honors, Honors, Honors

. . . splendor and majesty thou dost bestow upon her,
Yea, thou dost make her most blessed . . .

Psalms 21: 5,6

Retirement simply meant a change of work for Mrs. Glass. She moved from paid employment to a full life of volunteerism, lending her name and her talents to innumerable causes. When she speaks about the things that are most important to her, these priorities invariably surface:

- Texas College
- Home economics education
- Top Teens (a youth organization for African American youth)
- Anything for the improvement of Nacogdoches
- Community causes in Tyler

The retirement years have been filled with honors. The list is a long and impressive one, and the stories about how she came to be so honored are captivating. Mrs. Glass muses about some of them as friends talk together about the past. When visitors sit in her lovely living room filled with fine furniture and accessories, they are surrounded with evidence of her many honors. The plaques, pictures, and memorabilia overflow into the hall and other rooms. And someone listening quietly may overhear stories such as these.

· "When I retired, one of the gifts I got from friends was a trip to London. That was the first of the wonderful travels I had in the early retirement years. Probably my favorite was the trip to Equador with the International Women's Group."

"Maybe my highest honor was the honorary doctorate in Humane Letters I was given by Texas College on May 16, 1988."

· "Horace Johnson is a cousin of mine who served as a recruiter for UCLA's football program. Through Horace, I came to know the chancellor of UCLA, Dr. Young. He invited me to be his guest at the Rose Bowl Game in 1985. We had seats on the 50-yard line, and there were receptions and dinner parties for all the guests. I loved meeting the coaches, players and university administrators. What a fine time it was!"

· "The mayor of Los Angeles presented me with the Key to the City while I was there. You know Mayor Tom Bradley is a Texan, and his brother was working for Texas College at the time—he often drove my car; he was a fine helpful employee."

· "When I was named to the Texas Women's Hall of Fame, Governor Mark White treated all of us honorees like royalty. The receptions and dinner parties were exquisite. I had five suites in the Driskill Hotel for my family and friends. You know that hotel is one of those that had refused me service just a few years ago when I worked for the Texas Education Agency before integration. Being in that hotel during the week of the award ceremonies was a pleasant experience."

· "I suppose no honors are more gratifying than those from home. I treasure the honor of having Tyler proclaim a Willie Lee Campbell Day; and of course I loved being placed in the Nacogdoches Hall of Fame."

· "It's satisfying too, to know I am on the Foundation Board of Stephen F. Austin State University; that I have given a scholarship there; and that the First Profes-

Willie Lee Glass with Texas Governor Mark White.

Willie Lee Glass with Texas Governor Ann Richards.

On this day, September 9, 1997

Nacogdoches Citizens

established at

Stephen F. Austin State University

The E. J. Campbell Professorship in

Educational Leadership

to honor the life, work and leadership of

Professor Edward John Campbell

1877-1937

Present-day home of Willie Lee Glass in Tyler, Texas.

sorship in the College of Education carries Papa's name —all at a university where I was not permitted to study in the days before integration."

· "I've loved being honored by meeting the famous people who have been brought to Tyler for the Speakers Bureau: Henry Kissinger, Edward Teller, Larry King, Jack Kemp, Linda Bird Johnson, Coretta Scott King, Tipp O'Neill, Governor Ann Richards, Governor Mark White, Mayor Tom Bradley, John Eisenhower, Eleanor Roosevelt, and Liz Carpenter.

"I shall always be grateful to Dr. George F. Hamm, president of the University of Texas at Tyler, and others who made it possible for me to experience and enjoy many current educational updates on domestic and world affairs."

· "In the thanksgiving days of my life, I treasure the time I have to reflect on deeds, donations, counsel, and opportunities to honor the memory of the late Isadore Roosth, Joe Zeppa, Gus Taylor, Henry Bell, Sr., Dr. Edgar Vaughn, Benny Roosth, R. W. Fair, J. C. McAdams, Bishop R. A. Carter, Alex Woldert, Ralph Spence, Mrs. M.E.V. Hunter, Wilton Daniel, Watson Wise, Dr. Ivol Spafford, Dr. Bernice Moore, A. A. Arnold, Rev. D. C. Fowler, La Grellings, Judge Tom Rainey, Tom Burton, E. S. Sterling and others. As I reflect on the work of these giants of the past, I know that their sons and daughters represented by Dr. Jim Vaughn, Calvin Clyde, Dr. Jesse Jones, Norman Morehead, Judge Jack Pierce, James Perkins, Jerry Nasits, Marion Uphsaw, A. L. Mangham, C. L. Simon, Percy Simmons, Judge Harry Loftis, Harold Johnson, Dr. Charles Alexander, Luther Simond, Bill Hartley, Henry Bell, Jr., A. W. Riter, Walton P. Little, and others are carrying on their traditions of generosity and service to not only Texas College, but also to the entire Tyler and Texas community. They are legends that mirror the work of the legendary giants of the past."

DR. JONES TRIBUTE

The late Dr. John Paul Jones summarized Mrs. Glass' work in an article printed here with permission:

Circus Magic: Willie Lee Glass

Willie Lee Glass, by any measure, is a most remarkable woman. She came to Tyler in 1936, the blushing bride of Dr. D. R. Glass, president of Texas College. She was without connections or influence. Today she boasts of having served ten Texas governors across party lines, a personal relationship with Governor Ann Richards that began when the two were inducted together into the Texas Hall of Fame in 1985, and an invitation from the office of the late President Dwight D. Eisenhower to represent the state of Texas and the United States on an official people to people Travel Program delegation to Scandinavia, Poland and the Soviet Union to foster understanding between peoples of the world. Her phenomenal growth in personal influence came partly as a result of a fortunate juncture of time, place and person. Her own characteristics and attributes make it more likely that she would have risen to prominence at any time or place.

A great deal of her leadership ability could be justifiably attributed to the precepts and examples of her parents. It was her father, E. J. Campbell who was elected principal of the Nacogdoches colored high school in 1910, the year of her birth, and encouraged her to reach for the stars. The school was later named for her father.

Growing up as a campus brat, confident and privileged, Willie Lee went on to earn a B.S. degree in Home Economics at Prairie View A&M and a M.S. degree from Iowa State College, Ames, Iowa in 1933. Thus, from Iowa, fully equipped, she went to Virginia State College to head the Food and Nutrition Department in Home Economics.

After marriage and making her home in Tyler, she began an arduous schedule of activities as the helpmate of President Glass. Her personal rise to prominence resulted from several strands of development, sometimes separate, sometimes coordinated, sometimes intertwined, sometimes parallel, but always related: Education, fund raising, public relations, administration, building and intervention in desegregation.

Mrs. Glass' personality is complicated, fiercely proud at times and becomingly humble at others. She attributes her pride to her father's unstinting praise of her every action and her humility to her mother's unfailing efforts to keep her feet on the ground. For her enthusiasm, boundless energy, and her willingness to be useful, she credits both parents.

Somewhere along the way, Mrs. Glass developed an uncanny ability to judge people and to make the right friends. This added to an unusual ability to assess the probable and the possible in a situation.

One strand of her evolution was the development of important friendships and associations. Mr. and Mrs. Isadore Roosth found a source of help in Mrs. Glass when she provided assistance in the culinary arts and nutritional well-being of their family. Mrs. Glass and her students adopted the Roosths as a laboratory project. Mr. Roosth became a pillar of support to Texas College until his demise.

Mr. Joe Zeppa came to Tyler with an old country respect for farms and farming activities. He invited Mrs. Glass and her students to cater one of his social occasions in south Tyler. Preparations completed, he invited Mrs. Glass to join him and his guests. So efficient had been her preparations, and so charming and appropriate were her social graces that she became a respected lifelong friend to the Zeppas, with advantages to her program and her college.

Sitting in the office of Dr. Jim Vaughn for an eye appointment, Mrs. Glass became aware of a dilemma Dr. Vaughn was facing. He needed to acquire a substantial list of Smith County tax payers who favored the expansion of Medical Center Hospital. Mrs. Glass volunteered to help. Her list was so extensive that she ingratiated herself forever to the Vaughn family.

Her personal lifelong friendship with Mr. Walter Fair and his wife, Mattie, and others probably resulted from her continuing efforts to build bridges and to provide laboratory opportunities through catering for individuals and families in south Tyler.

From the beginning, in 1936, and on the basis of her experiences and associations, Mrs. Glass saw the need for organized fundraising efforts at Texas College. She organized annual class competitions for the honor of naming Homecoming queen, and in the process, developed relations with students and the football team. By 1944, she had initiated, directed, or prominently participated in fund raising projects: the annual United Negro College Fund drive, first college paved walkways and streets, a distinctive college entrance, a sprinkler system and an entry sign.

Mrs. Glass never lost sight of her goal of establishing a Home Economics Department with appropriate laboratories, approved and accredited. The modern, well-equipped building for Home Economics bears her name.

Her peers often say, "Willie Lee Glass clearly can't help but project a positive outlook." Her own philosophy in this regard is, "Black colleges need to concentrate on doing things well and be known for that. They should strive for excellence without excuse." And so the end of this recital.

Mrs. Glass' rise to prominence might be likened to a multi-ring circus that has only one star who must perform in all rings, sometimes separately, sometimes magically at the same time.

Rest and complete retirement are for others, but not for Willie Lee Glass. She still sits on important boards, 18 at present, including those of Stephen F. Austin State University, East Texas Medical Center, East Texas Lighthouse for the Blind, and UT Foundation. With a slightly slower step, she is still energetic and mentally active, still willing to be useful and serve, still ready for the next project, which has already been selected. Willie Lee Glass says her ultimate goal is to increase contributions to the United Negro College Fund. Would-be detractors would say that Mrs. Glass' rise to prominence was pure luck, a combination of time, place and person. Supporters look at who and what Mrs. Glass is and insist that she would have risen at any time and place.

Whatever questions others may have, Mrs. Glass is satisfied with her life. Plaques of recognition and honors line the walls of her home. These include the Texas Women's Hall of Fame (1985) and Zonta's Woman of the Year. Friends and former students visit her home daily to see that her wishes are met.

(From *The Tyler Morning Telegraph*)

IOWA STATE HONORS

On November 19, 1997, the following article honored Mrs. Glass, and is printed here with permission:

Latest Honors Reflect Well on Mrs. Glass, Tyler

Mrs. Willie Lee Glass no doubt is one of Tyler's most honored citizens, with the latest tribute being a Distinguished Achievement Citation from her alma mater, Iowa State University, on Oct. 24.

"You have made a significant contribution to the field of home economics education and, more importantly, in the area of civil rights," Martin Jischke, president of the alumni Awards Committee at Iowa State, said in notifying Mrs. Glass of the honor. "Your many friends and colleagues have great respect for what you have accomplished and the manner in which you do your work."

This is the second time Mrs. Glass has been honored by Iowa State. In 1971, she was selected as one of the school's distinguished alumnus recognized during a Home Economics Alumni Centennial Awards celebration.

She also has collected a long list of other honors in Tyler and East Texas and well beyond. National recognition came to her in 1972 when she was honored by National Business and Professional Women's clubs as Woman of the Year, and she also has been recognized by that group with its "Sojourner Truth" Award.

In Tyler, Mrs. Glass was a 1985 recipient of the annual T. B. Butler Award which recognizes outstanding citizens. She also was named Woman of the Year in 1985, and the same year was inducted into the Texas Woman's Hall of Fame by then Gov. Mark White. She was the honoree at the "People of Vision" dinner in Tyler in 1988.

Yet another recognition for Mrs. Glass is scheduled in Tyler today at the Third Annual Philanthropy Day Awards luncheon. She is one of five groups and individuals to be honored. She is cited as "Outstanding Volunteer Fund Raiser."

She has received Prairie View A&M's Distinguished Alumna Award, the school from which she received the B.S. degree in home economics before attending Iowa

Iowa State University Alumni Association Award

State. She also has done extensive study at Columbia University and Union Theological Seminary in New York.

Nacogdoches, of which she is a native, recognized Mrs. Glass in 1985 for contributions she made to that city and its residents. She was inducted into the Old Timers Breakfast Hall of Fame, a part of that city's annual Heritage Festival. A former educational adviser under 10 Texas governors, she was the first living inductee to the Nacogdoches group. Her father, the late E. J. Campbell, was a school principal for 26 years and community leader in that area. Among her contributions cited were land donations for an early childhood center and a community development program, and serving on a Stephen F. Austin State University advisory board.

Mrs. Glass also taught and led the home economics department at Texas College in Tyler, where her late husband, Dr. D. R. Glass was president. As a result of her leadership of the department there, a home economics building costing more than $300,000 was named in her honor.

In 1969, she was invited to attend the White House Conference on Children and Youth preparation held in Tulsa, Okla. And in 1981 she was appointed to the Texas board on Aging by then Gov. Bill Clements. At the Iowa State recognition last month, Mrs. Glass said: ". . . It was a long, long journey from a small rural community in East Texas to the campus of Iowa State University. But through the providence of God, the love of parents and the prayers of many, even dreams come true!

For me, it was at Iowa State that I embraced a life-defining experience that set the compass of my soul toward the farthest star. And, I have never looked back! I am therefore grateful to Iowa State University as well as other colleges and universities for preparing me and endowing me with a sense of personal commitment to render service to my fellow man."

And she added: "Moreover, God blessed me through the years to be identified with causes and movements that help mold the moral and spiritual fiber of our society. Not the least of these is Texas College where lies my heart and the very soul of my late husband, Dr. Dominion R. Glass, who served as its president for more than 30 years." It is easy to see from a review of her accomplishments that all of the honors accorded to Mrs. Glass are well deserved. They reflect well not only on the recipient, but also on the Tyler community.

The long record of service and contributions by Mrs. Glass in many areas is an example for others of how one person can have an impact and make a significant difference in a very positive way.

A unanimous "well done" is in order.

Chapter 10

Community Building

Behold, how good and how pleasant it is for brethren to dwell together in unity.

Psalms 133: 1

In Nacogdoches, Texas, when the name E. J. Campbell is mentioned, someone who is old enough to remember times before integration will invariably comment on Professor Campbell's role as a mediator in relations between the whites and the blacks. They may go on to speak of his work as an educational leader, but they insist that his greatest contribution to the town was his community building activity.

He was a member of every board that involved both races. For example, he was always the chair of the Red Cross Drive in the black community. It was Mr. Campbell who was called when the sheriff had problems with anyone from the black community, just as it was Mr. Campbell and Dr. Nelson who were called in when there was any sign of an erupting conflict between the races.

Community problems or community opportunities, Professor and Mrs. Campbell were involved. And they communicated the importance of that involvement to their daughter.

MRS. GLASS' COMMUNITY WORK

To cite Mrs. Glass' first community work is as futile as to try to cite the appearance of the first pine tree in her beloved East Texas. She has always been a part of the community and its work. As a child and youth, the work centered around school and church. Away at school, her involvement was focused on student organizations. But as an adult, she has spent seventy years building community wherever she lives and works.

CIVIC ORGANIZATIONS

There were numerous civic and social organizations that Mrs. Glass had a large stake in, either as founder, co-founder, or as an interested and dedicated member. She played major leadership roles in helping the group clarify their mission and in planning ways their work would benefit the general community.

One of the organizations was Alpha Kappa Alpa Sorority, Inc. Having been initiated into the Beta Gamma chapter at Des Moines, Iowa, during her graduate study at Iowa State College, Mrs. Glass realized that all undergraduate coeds could profit from the organization. At Texas College at Tyler she was able to establish a chapter.

Because Willie Lee wanted the best of everything for students at Texas College, she was concerned with extracurricular activities as well as with academics. In her quest for establishing the AKA sorority on campus, she was equally interested in having all sororities and fraternities accessible to students. Therefore, she worked cooperatively with Dr. George N. Redd, academic dean of Texas College, to bring Greekdom to the campus. Dr. Redd brought the first fraternity, Kappa Alpha Psi, to the campus, followed by the AKA sorority. Shortly, the Panhellenic Council was established. Lyceum programs, Vespers, convocations and fundraising events that were scheduled on campus were significantly augmented both physically and financially by the helpful participation of these Greek organizations. Soon Mrs. Glass and others helped the AKA sorority purchase a sorority house. The City of Tyler sold the old Ella Reed Negro Library Building to the local alumni chapter, Gamma Omicron Omega, for the house. It is used today as a service center for the community. There are two surviving charter members of the Gamma Omicron Omega chapter: Willie Lee Glass and Julia B. Warren.

One person interviewed for this book related a story that illustrates Mrs. Glass' caring attitude toward students and staff. Soon after she arrived at Texas College as first lady, a coed became suddenly ill in the dormitory on Saturday night while a school social (dance) was being held in the Redding Room of Phillips Hall, a girls dormitory. Two students were sent to the president's home to use the telephone to call Dr. Warren, the school physician. Unfortunately, Dr. Warren and President Glass were in Chicago attending a church meeting. Mrs. Glass overheard the conversation of the girls and she rushed immediately to the dormitory to check with the dean of women, Mrs. Patton, to see what was being done for the sick student.

Mrs. Patton informed Mrs. Glass that it was policy to use only the school physician; therefore, she could not call another doctor. Mrs. Glass said, "I can." Mrs. Patton asked, "Who will pay for the service?" Mrs. Glass said, "I will," and proceeded to call a specialist who came immediately. Unfortunately, it was too late to save the young coed. She died in Mrs. Glass' arms. Of course, this act of kindness and bravery endeared the first lady to students and parents alike. John Stephenson, pharmacist, frequently recounted the many times Mrs. Glass would pay for student medications from her own savings.

It was about a year or two after Mrs. Glass' arrival at Tyler to live as the wife of the college president that she met several prominent and influential families. Mrs. Glass lost no time in telling and selling her story of home economics and soliciting their help in developing her departmental programs. Mr. W. Wise, a prominent businessman, made a special request of Mrs. Glass to always send a student to his home during the Rose Festival to help receive the guests. Gloria Todd, a very talented student in the fine arts, was sent time after time. Mr. Wise said, "Her voice was simply melodious and she has the talent to perform the hostess role perfectly."

Mrs. Glass recruited many supporters for Texas College. One was Mrs. Gertrude Zeppa, a major supporter, mentor, advisor, and benefactor of the Texas College program. She was generous financially as well as with other resources necessary for the balancing of a strong and functional home economics program. These resources included home furnishings, special equipment, accessories, and other accouterments. Mrs. Zeppa's expertise in the culinary art realm made a perfect match with the teachers of home economics at Texas College. The experimentation and creative preparation of foods paid off quite well for both parties. Mrs. Zeppa worked closely with LaVerne R. Madlock, Margaret E. Surry Fingal, the late Freddie Moody and Lillie Mae Claybon, and other staff members. Mrs. Adeline Stuckey Sikes also contributed her talents and other resources to the Texas College program in general.

President Glass and Mrs. Glass subscribed to the practice of growing their own faculty. Many graduates of Texas College continued graduate studies and returned to campus with higher degrees to help move the institution forward. Cases in point were Dr. Jesse Jones, Mabel Baxter Tucker, LaVerne Madlock, and Margaret Fingal. Some graduates began and finished their study career in home economics and then chose other work, but they continued to maintain a healthy and positive relationship with Texas College and Mrs. Glass. Mrs. Glass cited these students and graduates who represent those willing and ready to aid and champion any endeavor relative to the ongoing of Texas College. She says there are many, many others too numerous to name.

Margaret Elam
Gadys M. Square, ex-city councilwoman
Vernice C. Melontree, elementary teacher
Bernice M. McKay, home demonstration specialist

Ernestine C. Ashford, home economist/adult education
Espie Johnson, caterist
Darlene Lewis, home economist
Dr. Lucilla Marks, home economist
Ella Grace Turner, business
Ella Fay Perry, Head Start director/consultant
Ella Mae White Smith, home economist
Helen Brewer, home economist, retired
Erce Hodge, principal and home economist
Margie H. Riley, principal and home economist
Lillian Williams
Beulah Jones, principal and home economist
Betty Lou McNeal, principal and home economist
Dale Henderson
Miriam R. King
Violet Clark, home economist
Mary O. Reel, home economist
Pearl W. Wells, principal and home economist
Mary Freeman
Odessa Preston Sanders, principal and home economist
Odell Everhart, principal and home economist
Lillian Kissam, principal and home economist

When Mrs. Glass accepted the position of consultant with the Texas Education Agency, LaVerne Madlock, a graduate of Texas College and Iowa State College, was named to replace her as director of home economics at Texas College. Mrs. Madlock had the prestigious diploma in culinary art from New York, N.Y., and had a brief stint with the Extension Service and an apprenticeship at the Zodiac Room in Neiman Marcus, Dallas, with Helen Corbett. She was also a recipient of the Dansforth Scholarship.

The famous Texas College Tea House, designed and managed by Mrs. Madlock, was a visible part of the Home Economics Program, and it was used as a laboratory for preparing students in the field of institutional management and in culinary art. Mrs. Glass was particularly pleased that it helped to put and keep the home economics program "on the map."

Mrs. Glass also worked diligently to get vocational certification for the Home Economics Department. Authorities in Austin said that no other existing college in the state would be giving vocational certification for home economics. This meant schools not approved would have to send students to Prairie View or other schools for additional study in order to meet requirements and qualify as a vocational home economics teacher. But Mrs. Glass and her staff negotiated with the TEA people, and after more hard work and preparation the program was certified in 1950.

IN NACOGDOCHES

One could consider Mrs. Glass' community as Nacogdoches, Texas, where she maintains accounts in every bank, where she retains church membership, where she serves on boards of Stephen F. Austin State University, the E. J. Campbell Alumni Association, and many others. It is in Nacogdoches that the fine Head Start Building stands on land she gave the community for the establishment of this program for children and their families.

IN TYLER

Or one may consider Mrs. Glass' community as Tyler, Texas, where she works with the schools, college, fire department, civic center, United Way, Chamber of Commerce, and other organizations. In fact, recently Mrs. Glass was honored by the City of Tyler as a Distinguished Philanthropist.

Her work has always shown no barriers, for while Texas College has been her first priority, she has worked in all areas of Tyler's community life. For example, some years ago Tyler needed to strengthen its program for people who are physically challenged. Of course, leaders called Mrs. Glass for her help. Strategies were developed, work began, and it was not surprising a few months later to see a picture in the Tyler papers of Mrs. Glass and others cutting the ribbon for the opening of a new Goodwill Building in the city.

The North Tyler Neighborhood Improvement Association has profited from her work. With both Texas College and her home in the area, she is a natural leader for the group that works to improve the community.

To name the Tyler Boards on which Mrs. Glass serves is to create an impressive list. However, she has consistently prioritized her work in the area of education, health, and public welfare. For example, she is on the board of trustees of Texas College and on the board of directors for The University of Texas, Tyler. Her work for the United Negro College Fund has resulted in impressive amounts of money for scholarships.

She is a director on the board of the Medical Center Hospital in Tyler, and she has lent her fundraising skills to work for the establishment of the Tyler Vision Center and for the Tyler Breast Center.

Her work with Fire Department fundraising and development is well known. There is little wonder at her recent award as a philanthropist in Tyler.

THE STATE

From another perspective, Mrs. Glass' community may be the whole state of Texas' vast educational system. Teacher, leader, consultant, member of advisory boards, and champion advocate, there is no part of education that escapes her interest.

She has long served on advisory boards for curriculum in family studies.

In the 1970s, when the challenges of integration were at their height, she worked across the state with teachers on solutions for the problems they might encounter. The following illustrates the scope of the problems she helped teachers face:

- Why are minority students so reluctant to ask for help from teachers?
- How can a teacher tactfully help a child to see that using "color" as a crutch to try to prevent class cor-

rections is not the proper thing to do in any situation?

- How may teachers encourage sharing of customs among students?
- How can we promote the understanding that improved standards of living is the result of work, not gifts?
- How do we help students develop more self-discipline?
- What discipline problems can we expect with more differences in the classroom?
- How does a teacher react to the continuous mumbling of minority students during class?
- How does a teacher cope with students' striving for attention?
- How can we help public school students of minority races overcome the feeling of hostility toward the Anglo race?
- How may we help students improve their appearance without hurting their feelings?
- How may we help students improve their spoken language?
- How may we get students to "talk out their problems" rather than "act out" them?
- How do we prevent students from segregating themselves?
- What is the reaction to touching from a teacher?
- If black students do not like something, they refuse to do it at all. How to cope?
- How do we teach eye-to-eye contact during conversation?
- How can teachers prevent minority feelings of unfairness from simple mistakes in the classroom?
- How can we teach more careful listening and following directions?

TOP LADIES OF DISTINCTION

Mrs. Glass joined other strong black women to found

an organization that has had a major impact on women and youth. Called Top Ladies of Distinction, Inc., it was established in the early 1960s.

Women from many nations who had achieved distinction in either culture, education, business, finance, or community service were invited to join the organization. The women represented a cross-section of human resources with a potpourri of special talents and skills. Major Ozell Dean was one of the women.

Major Dean was a graduate of Texas College in Tyler, and she contacted three of her Tyler friends to talk with them about the possibilities of establishing the organization for black girls and women. Four women, Mrs. Franchell Boswell, Mrs. LaVerne Madlock, Mrs. Georgia Bell Presswood, and Mrs. Augusta Cash, met in June 1964 with Mrs. Glass at her office at Texas College. From the beginning they held the idea that they would work together to promote top achievement among women with the focus on top service. They would focus on teens, senior citizens, community beautification, and improving the status of women.

As a result of that meeting in Tyler, they organized the Top Ladies of Distinction. They saw themselves as people who would concentrate efforts to alleviate moral and social problems in the youth of the day. Their main goal would be to help youth function effectively in today's society. More specifically, helping youth command the social graces and appreciate the dignity of work was their major concern.

The national organization of Top Ladies of Distinction was incorporated under the laws of the state of Texas, September 8, 1964, with the following chartered members: Mrs. Willie Lee Glass, Tyler; Mrs. Franchell Boswell; Dr. Ina Bolton Brown, Houston; Mrs. Augusta Cash, Memphis; Major Ozelle Dean, Washington, D.C.; Mrs. LaVerne Madlock, Tyler; Mrs. Ruth Payne, Navasota; and Mrs. George Prestwood, Dallas.

Their first meeting was hosted by Mrs. Glass, Mrs. Boswell, and Mrs. Madlock in Tyler, June 4, 1965. From the onset, helping youth was the priority of the women. Mrs. Madlock said, "We absolutely had to get the young black women ready to function effectively in integrated schools and society." Mrs. Glass, in her role as Texas Education Agency consultant, was a natural for leading the effort in Texas, as well as for serving on the national board.

The first Top Ladies of Distinction out-of-state chapter was established by Mrs. Glass as women in other states picked up the idea of organizing to support black women and youth who were working to reach their potential.

The women sponsored an organization for black youth, called Top Teens of Distinction. The group embraced the old African proverb, "Children are the reward of Life." Each of the founders published their philosophy of life to be used in mentoring teens. Mrs. Glass stated this philosophy: "To be tops in service to all mankind and especially to the youth of the land. Service is the rent we pay for living in God's world. We must live with change. Remember that Columbus was months crossing the Atlantic; then Lindbergh crossed it in thirty-three hours; and Astronaut White crossed it in fourteen minutes." Her advice to Top Teens was in the same vein of thought: "Make good today—do not worry about tomorrow; God is already there."

The leaders cited the following poem by an unknown author as an inspiration for their mentoring program:

I dreamed I stood in a studio
   and watched two sculptors there.
The clay they used was a young child's mind
   And they fashioned it with care.
One was a teacher; the tools he used
   Were books and music and art.
One a parent with a guiding hand
   And a gentle, loving heart.
Day after day, the teacher toiled
   With a touch that was deft and sure.
While the parent labored by his side

And polished and smoothed it o'er.
And, when at last their task was done
They were proud of what they had wrought.
For the things they had molded into the child
Could neither be sold nor bought.
And each agreed he would have failed
If he had worked alone.
For, behind the parent stood the school,
And behind the teacher, the home.

Leaders describe the mentoring program as one that mentors, protects, nurtures, teaches, and serves. The following poem, published in the 1997 Top Ladies of Distinction, Inc., & Top Teens of America Annual Program Booklet, is testimony to the success of the mentoring efforts. The poem was written by Teen Bernest Lott of the San Antonio Metropolitan Chapter:

They lead us through the tunnels of life,
whenever we are lost.
And teach us responsibility
when it's time to pay the cost.
Although sometimes we don't listen,
we still know who's the boss.
And they tell us we are children of God
when history says we were bought.
Now these women have been here
to make our days bright when we felt blue.
They have been answers to our questions
when before we had no clue.
Who could you call on
when you had no one else to talk to?
To the Top Ladies of Distinction Mentors,
we all thank you.

Today the organization continues the tradition begun by Mrs. Glass and those early leaders. Its national theme for 1997 was "Mentoring—Nurturing—Collaboration: Strengthening the Village."

Mrs. Glass' work with Top Ladies of Distinction and Top Teens continues today. She has spent years helping establish chapters in towns across Texas and states across the nation. Her work in providing workshops for youth is recognized as some of the most vital programming during the years of transition. And today she continues to serve as a mentor to young women.

The work of Top Ladies has become legendary across Texas and across the nation, because each woman pledges to be tops in whatever she does, and each pledges herself to work for community, youth, senior citizens, and improved status of women. The following words are excerpted from a personal report one Top Lady wrote to her mentor:

> I am listing three things I have done to strengthen the village since SYN LOD. (1997 annual convocation):
>
> 1. Took care of a three-week-old baby after his mother became violently ill and had to be rushed to the hospital emergency.
> 2. Took time to drive a 92 year old neighbor to the Social Security Office to have his deceased wife's check replaced in his name.
> 3. Carried reading materials to a Senior Disabled Center for the residents to read. The magazines were *Forbes*, *Jet*, *People*, and *Ebony*.

MENTAL FASHIONS

Among the many workshops Mrs. Glass developed and gave for young women and for teachers across the country was a most popular one called "Mental Fashions for the '70s." In the workshop Mrs. Glass focused on the role and power of attitude in reaching goals and in learning to live in an integrated society. The format of this workshop was appealing to her audience for it was a format they related to because of the frequent fashion shows presented by the home economics teachers and their clothing students. The presentation follows.

Why a Mental Fashion Show?

America as it begins the seventies reveals that we continue living in an age of unrest, in an age of violence, of changing philosophies, manners, and morals. We live closer together, but feel more apart, for there can be great loneliness in a crowd. We live in an age of contrasts. For those who have eyes to see, the signs are manifest: signs of plenty and signs of poverty; signs of enduring and changing values; signs of opportunity and signs of despair.

Mental fashion as a social phenomenon reflects the cultural environment and satisfies existing needs, while in turn promotes new attitudes and values. The changing form of mental fashion is largely determined by challenges to conform or to assert individuality and by social and economic conditions of society.

Though you may be unaware of it, possibly because of concentration on physical fashion, your mental fashion has played an important role in creating you. Mental fashion is still influencing your thinking, feeling, and acting each day of your life.

All of us are aware that each individual wants to have an identity. He wants to answer the proverbial question—"Who am I?" A formula to help answer the question cannot be given, for each human being is unique and must find his or her own answers. But a mental fashion show is a means of helping an individual discover self. The goal of this presentation is to reveal what happens when each member of an audience such as ours unlocks the mind and delves into its recesses to study the combinations of mental garments with which the environments and experiences have clothed that unique mind.

The Need for Blending Physical and Mental Fashions

If money as it relates to being best dressed means anything, then the American teen should truly be recognized as one of the best dressed teens in the world. A study made by the Youth Research Institute indicates that teens spent 30 billion dollars during a recent year. And the greater percentages of that is on such things as clothes, costume jewelry, grooming aids, gasoline, and movies.

Much of this buying is prompted by teen insecurity, resulting from what one writer has described as a network of anxiety whose chief terrors are loneliness and pimples. Some teens buy anything. What it is does not matter so long as it satisfies the ego and eases frustrations. Others buy for status.

Not only are dollars—billions of them—spent annually, but also a vast amount of time and energy are spent selecting the wardrobe for the outer you. But what of the inner you? No high fashion designer, no amount of jewelry, no fashionable hair style, can develop a genuinely beautiful inner you. You must be as concerned about the person who dwells within your body as you are about the trappings you put on your body. For genuine beauty within and without, an individual's mental wardrobe and the necessary accessories must be comparable to the exotic and exquisite fabrics and designs that make up high fashion.

The inner you and the outer you are the whole you and should be carefully correlated. A tired accessory can spoil a costume, but a mind full of unhealthy thoughts and attitudes can spoil an entire wardrobe.

Consider the mental fashions that are about to be illustrated and think of your own mental wardrobe. Ask yourself if it shows more than a few pardonable mistakes. Resist the temptation to hold on to those mental fashions and accessories that yield a harvest of undesirable qualities. Rather, select the ones that will make a beautiful you. Discard all the others!

Here, then, are the mental fashions for this year and for any year of successful living:

COURAGE: The strength of a right-minded right-acting person.

Courage is that quality of mind which meets danger or opposition with calmness and firmness. Life is a voyage in which we choose neither vessel nor weather, but much can be done in the management of the sails and the guidance of the helm.

Freddie Steinmark [a man in the news at the time, who suffered great tribulation in his life] exhibits courage in his attitude toward life. He has shown that he is not the victim of his circumstances, but the master of them.

PREJUDICE: The cancer of the human soul.

Unchecked, prejudice grows to overpower both the mind and the heart. Albert Hatcher, writing in *The New Republic,* "Negro Youth and College," November 9, 1942, said,

If you discriminate against me because I am uncouth, I can become mannerly. If you ostracize me because I am unclean, I can cleanse myself. If you segregate me because I lack knowledge, I can become educated. But if you discriminate against me because of my color, I can do nothing; God gave me my color.

DESPAIR: The spiritual feet dragging in the mud, sometimes despite all personal effort.

If we fill our hours with regrets over the failures of yesterday and with worries over the problems of tomorrow, we have only today in which to be thankful.

When the storms of life rage, do as the eagle who sets his wings, faces the storm, and immediately goes up, up, up above the storm. He faces the storm and uses it to rise to new heights.

Do you see difficulties in every opportunity or opportunities in every difficulty? No man ever injured his eyesight by looking on the bright side of things.

HOPE: The exuberance of the healthy soul.

Wilfred A. Peterson said, "While there is hope, there is life. Hope comes first; life follows. Hope rouses life to continue, to expand, to grow, to reach out, to go on. Hope sees a light where there isn't any. Hope lights candles in millions of despairing hearts. Hope never sounds retreat. Hope keeps the banners flying. Hope revives ideals, renews dreams, revitalizes visions. Hope scales peaks, wrestles with the impossible, achieves the highest aims. As long as man has hope, no situation is hopeless."

HATE: A prolonged manner of suicide.

Hate is the aggressive person's drop-out pattern. Life is too short to be little. Toss out hatred; fill its place with love. Love is not soft; it is hard like a rock on which the waves of hatred beat in vain.

Malice, hot anger and sullen hate, scorn of the lowly

and envy of the great will do more harm to the person who is hating than to the object of hate.

PRIDE: A reasonable delight in one's position, achievements, and possessions. It also refers to lofty self-respect.

One of the biggest thrills in life comes from doing a job well. Be a lamp in the chamber if you cannot be a star in the sky. You have no idea of the impact of your image and example on those persons whose lives you touch. Your guidelines for pride should be directed by God's teachings.

ENVY: Self-inflicted torture.

The secret of contentment lies in our ability to enjoy what we have and to lose all desire for things beyond our reach.

Each new day is an opportunity to start all over again —to cleanse our minds and hearts anew and to clarify our vision. Let us not clutter up today with the leavings of other days.

Envy is a corroding, all pervasive jealousy that poisons every human relationship. It is the discontent which a person develops because of his resentment of the excellence or good fortune of another. It is a cry for love.

ANGER: Frustration breaking out and losing control.

Anger is the emotion of displeasure, and usually antagonism, excited by a sense of injury or insult.

When we give in to anger, the situation controls us, the other person has the upper hand, and we spend much of our time hating ourselves and hating the other person involved.

Dr. Norman Vincent Peale's antidote for anger is to fill the mind with attitudes of good will, forgiveness, love, and the spirit of imperturbability.

Let us realize that what happens around us is largely outside our control, but that the way we choose to react to it is inside our control.

HAPPINESS: Love's result.

To be happy ourselves is a most effectual contribution to the happiness of others.

Happiness is not a station at which you arrive, but a manner of traveling. The amount of happiness in your life depends on the quality of your thoughts. Happiness is a running stream, not a stagnant pool.

Be cheerful. Of all things you wear, your expression is the most important.

FAITH: A rock; the substance of things hoped for, the evidence of things unseen.

One can be aware of faith as easily as one can be aware of the earth. Faith is as certain as the taste of an apple, the fragrance of a rose, the sound of thunder, the sight of the sun, the feel of a loving touch.

Great people are not affected by each puff of wind that blows ill. Like great ships, they sail serenely on, in a calm sea or a great tempest.

LOVE: A deep desire to know and understand and serve mankind, recognizing that everybody is somebody.

Love has many faces. In the words of the Apostle Paul found in the New Testament, "it suffers long and is kind; it envies not; it flaunts not itself; it behaves itself not unseemly; it seeks not its own; it is not easily provoked; it rejoices in the truth; it bears all things, believes all things, hopes all things, endures all things. Love never fails."

Love is the passionate and abiding desire on the part of two or more people to produce together conditions under which each can be, and spontaneously express, his real self; to produce together an intellectual soil and emotional climate in which each can flourish, far superior to what either could achieve alone.

Love produces a desire to know, to understand, to hug and be responsible for another person.

To summarize, we may say that:

We cannot control the length of our lives—but we can control the width and depth. We cannot control the contour of our faces—but we can control the expression. We cannot control the weather—but we can control the atmosphere of our minds.

> Life should be sipped, not gulped. It should be savored for the love and kindness and happiness there is in it—for the beauty and goodness and opportunities for spiritual unfoldment it holds. Right now you can have the time of your life.
>
> Our scrutiny of mental fashions should lead to a greater understanding of the apparel which we should retain and enhance and of that which we should immediately discard because of its destructive nature to the human soul. All these mental symbols are but an attitude toward life. The symbols, desirable or undesirable, give an illusion of one's image. Let us take the wholesome and enhancing garments of our mental wardrobes and use them as guideposts for living as we travel the highway of life.

FUNDRAISING

Co-workers and community leaders in Tyler say that Mrs. Glass is the most inspired fundraiser they have ever known. Over the years her creativity in planning strategies has amazed professionals in the field.

She began by using her father's methods of quietly but powerfully making a need known to people who had the interest and the resources for meeting the need. But later she developed a whole inventory of strategies. They included the famous Texas College Tea Room, where students served the Tyler community and their guests. Profits from the Tea Room added impressive dollars to the Texas College coffers. Home economics students managed the concession stands at every Texas College athletic event, and according to Mrs. Glass, "We sold anything that people would eat—hamburgers, hotdogs, pickles, chips, cookies, cakes, ice cream, gum, candy." Other strategies included raffles of all sorts. Once she led a group who raffled a new car for a charity event. At Mrs. Glass' suggestion the lucky winner sold the car and with the proceeds bought a house, which in turn was raffled. The dollars poured in!

At a formal banquet that was held at Texas College to

promote scholarships, Mrs. Glass asked each woman present if she would give the price of a new Easter outfit to the scholarship fund. "My last new outfit cost $400," she admitted, "and I know many of you buy more expensive clothing than I do. I challenge you to forego the next suit you are thinking of buying and instead give those funds to Texas College!" Again the dollars poured in!

When the Home Economics Building was under construction, Mrs. Glass organized a group to sell bricks for the building.

Mrs. Glass spent years working as a fundraiser for Texas College, but her work did not stop there. Way back in her first job in Virginia, she raised money to buy shoes for children in the Child Care Center. Through the years many groups have profited from her expertise as a fund raiser: child care centers, Top Teens, boys and girls clubs, the Firemen's Association, health centers, the United Negro College Fund, Head Start, churches, community centers. All these are representative of the groups she has helped.

She was great at soliciting gifts from merchants as a way of leveraging the profits from the fundraisers. For example, she always was able to get the drinks that were sold at the concession stands donated by a soft drink dealer. "I've never hesitated to ask people to help others in need," she says, "for when people care, they share. And caring for others enriches everyone!"

"Back in the forties," she mused, "we worked to improve the condition of homes in rural areas. Each year my classes would renovate one family home in the community. We added closets, painted, made cabinets for the kitchen, used orange crates and other resources as we could get them, to improve the home for the particular family. Of course, at the same time, the home economics students learned how to improve their own homes."

CHAPTER 11

"Papa and Mama Said . . ."

What is man that thou art mindful of him, and the son of man that thou dost care for him . . . thou hast made him little less than God, and dost crown him with glory and honor. Thou hast given him dominion over the works of thy hands; thou hast put all things under his feet.

Psalms 8:4-6

Willie Lee learned through repetition—her mother and father had sayings for just about every subject. They all are worth repeating.

"There are no black people, nor white people; we are all just different shades of brown."

"When you know, you care, and when you care, you will share."

"Never accept a job for only one year; stay at least two so people will know you could stay on the job if you wanted to."

"A meal without hot biscuits is not worth eating."

"Don't let a man give you advice on how to buy a saddle if he doesn't own a horse."

"Never go anywhere without a ticket home in your pocket.

"Be on time; the game may be won in the first inning."

"Beauty is God expressing himself."

"Dream big dreams; then put on your overalls."

"Chop your own wood, and it will keep you warm twice."

"You're not fully dressed until you put on a smile."

"Save some of every dollar you earn."

"Keep some money in every bank in town; money is power."

"If you want to help someone, help him like himself better."

"Always strive for excellence without excuses."

"Don't get angry; think; with anger you cannot think clearly, and you will probably lose the battle."

"A good man is too noble for anger; too courageous for doubt; and too full of God's love to hate."

"I'm always proud of my little girl."

"Wear a cap with your basketball uniform so you won't catch a cold."

"If I can get one foot in the door, you can be sure I'll get the other one in."

"You may have to work twice as hard as a white person, but you can do it; hard work pays."

"Everybody can be good at something."

"Everybody is someone special; deal with every individual with respect."

"When you have a task before you, learn all you can about it, then practice, practice, practice."

"Leave nothing to chance; prepare yourself to perform with excellence."

"Take positive action, not defensive action."

"Never, never, never let yourself get into a fight."

"Prejudice is the cancer of the soul."

"Envy is just self-inflicted torture."

"You can't pour perfume on someone else without getting a little on yourself."

"Life is too short to be little."

"Love is not soft; it's hard as a rock."

"Contentment is being able to enjoy what we have without longing for things beyond our reach."

"Willie Lee, every new day is a chance to start over."

"When you give in to anger, you lose control."

"Remember what Mama says, 'Your expression is the most important thing you wear.'"

"Great people aren't affected by every puff of wind that blows."

"Savor life for all the love and kindness and happiness you can experience in it."

"A quitter never wins, and a winner never quits."

"The only way you will ever have friends is to be a good friend."

"Cowards lie; strong people tell the truth."

"Study and prepare yourself so you will be ready when opportunity knocks."

"If your head is too big, you may not be able to get into a good opening."

"The emptier the pot, the quicker it boils."

"Be yourself if you ever hope to be somebody."

"Don't wait to be a great man—be a great boy."

"Oversleeping will never make your dreams come true."

"If you want to do something successful, you must do something else first."

"If you want to be successful, stay close to your maker."

"If you want to fix your feet, fix your head first."

THE CHARACTERISTICS PAPA TAUGHT TO WILLIE LEE

Willie Lee said Papa believed in twelve things so strongly that he required her to be able to recite them and practice saying them. The twelve are:

- The value of time.
- The pleasure of working.
- The need for persistence.
- The worth of good character.
- The joy of creating.
- The improvement of your own talent.
- The virtue of patience.
- The wisdom of economy.
- The obligation of duty.
- The importance of being a model.

- The power of kindness.
- The dignity found in simplicity.

PAPA'S DESCRIPTION OF GOOD LEADERS

A good leader is DEPENDABLE. You assume responsibilities and take them seriously if you want to be an effective leader. Carry out jobs well and get them done on time.

A good leader is EFFICIENT. You manage time well; recognize the value of making thorough preparation for tasks and plans so that important issues are not sidetracked or lost in the haze of unrelated ideas.

A good leader is SOCIABLE. To lead you must be able to get along well with people; you are sensitive to their feelings and are genuinely interested in their well-being.

A good leader is an effective COMMUNICATOR. Convey ideas and thoughts clearly to others; cultivate a strong but pleasant voice.

A good leader is a STABLE PERSON. You have poise and self-confidence; meet different situations tactfully and easily, controlling your emotions.

A good leader exerts SCHOLASTIC ABILITY. Good leaders are lifelong learners.

A good leader is PRESENTABLE. You are neat, tastefully dressed, and well-groomed as a sign of respect for yourself, for your organization, and for those you lead.

A good leader is DEDICATED. You believe in the goals of your organization, understanding the program of work, and interpret it to others.

Appendix

Excerpts from Teaching Files

(Lesson plans from Willie Lee Campbell Glass' files selected by her for "The Time of Transition.")

EXERCISE IN UNDERSTANDING MINORITIES

"You are a Nobody, You come from Nowhere, and you are going Nowhere."

Think carefully about the above statement.

How does it affect you?

Does it give you a comfortable feeling?

If not, you understand why we should learn more about and teach minorities.

Each minority receives the above message — if not overtly, then subtly.

What are you doing to help these people have a good image of themselves? The attitudes you promote will follow your students all of their lives.

Our nation is in danger of being destroyed by a powerful weapon—the attitudes and misunderstandings of people.

Struggle with and often change their attitudes toward the minorities. Set the stage for learning positive attitudes about roles of mankind. Engage a battle against negative attitudes by having students become aware of the likenesses of people through learning and understanding the structure of the human family. From the awareness of likenesses and similar needs and wants among people who are familiar, the child will be able to relate how people are dependent upon each other for existence.

Children should learn early scientific names, physical characteristics, and colors of the races of mankind. When children accept these facts as truths they will be capable of destroying the myths and prejudices of our past.

I. Concept: Families are alike (for Kindergarten)
   Generalization:
   A. Children need to become aware of the likenesses in family structure of all mankind.
   B. Able families have similar needs and wants.
   C. The differences in human behavior are understandable as variations in learned patterns of social behavior.
   D. Children should become acquainted with the scientific concept of color and what causes different colors in people.
   E. Children should be exposed to the characteristics in people that are inherited and how these characteristics are unique and desirable in all individuals.

II. Behavioral Goals
   A. Children will match people in the "People Game" to form sets of: size—large, small, tall, short; likenesses—boys, girls, children, men, women, age, etc.; number concepts—few, many, etc.; eyes, color differences.
   B. Children will group people into families on the flannel board and discuss how they are alike. Children will write a story about the people in the "People Game." Record all responses on a chart.

C. Children will be shown pictures of different racial families engaged in different activities. They will be asked to generalize what they think all families enjoy doing together.

D. Children will listen to a story to become aware of what makes color in man.

Suggested books:

The Story of Skin Color: Red Man, White Man, African Chief. Marguerite Lerner, M.D., Lerner Publication, 1960.

Grevious, Saundrah Black. *Teaching Children and Adults to Understand Human and Race Relations.* Minneapolis, MN: T.S. Denison, 1968.

E. Children will learn the scientific names and the physical characteristics of the Negroid, Mongoloid, and Caucasoid races.

F. Children will experiment with food coloring to understand the chemical melanin and carotene which cause coloring in the skin.

G. Children will discuss filmstrips and movies which show family life and needs of different racial families. Children will listen to stories and poems and will learn songs about these people.

H. Children will draw pictures and make a mural of all families and their activities.

I. Children will make stick puppets and act out different family activities. A family of each racial group should be represented.

III. Suggested Procedure

Opener (Setting the Stage for Learning)

"PEOPLE GAME"

Materials: A flannel board with about twenty to twenty-five people. These people are to have faces representing colors of different racial groups.

Teacher: Today we are going to play a game called the

"People Game." Who can find something alike about these people? Will you put these people together on the flannel board?

Child's Response: Child might choose grouping of men to begin.

Teacher: How are these men alike?

Child's Response: They are all daddies. They are all men. They all wear pants.

Teacher: Reads *The Story of Skin Color.*

Teacher: Yesterday we read a story about chemicals which make color (display a card labeled MELANIN). This chemical is found in the skin of men. Who remembers what color this chemical gives to the skin? Yes, melanin gives a brown color to skin.

Use the family group in the "People Game." Review the three basic racial names with children again and let them again group each family. If one family has members overlapping in skin color—good. Excellent opportunity to teach about racially mixed people. The following exercise will show the children how extremely difficult it is to distinguish the race of many people by their skin coloring.

Teacher: What did we find out about the color of people from our experimentation?

Culminating Activities: The teacher may wish to do several activities such as making a mural showing families and their activities or making stick puppets of family activities.

Evaluation:

1. Can children match groups of people in the "People Game"?
2. Do children understand that people can be families and that these families are different sizes and shades of color?
3. Do children understand that all families are alike, that they all have similar needs and wants?
4. Do children understand that all families are dependent upon each other?

5. Do children have some knowledge of the scientific names, physical characteristics of the Negroid, Mongoloid, and Caucasoid races?
6. Do children understand what causes the color in man?
7. Can children express how all families are alike by their participation in one or both of the culminating activities?

Content: Facts for Teachers Information

The three basic racial groups of people classified according to certain physical features are Negroid, Mongoloid, and Caucasoid races.

The Negroid race includes the American Negro or Afro-American, the African (Pigmy Watusi, Ethiopians, Sudanese, etc.), Haitian, mixed persons, etc.

Teacher: These are pictures of families. All these people have amounts of the chemical melanin which makes their skin various shades of color. Melanin is a chemical which gives a brown color to the skin. Do all these people have the same color skin? These are pictures of Negroid families. (Show pictures of Negroid family with dark brown coloring to their skin.) These people in this picture have lots of melanin in their skin. That's why they have skin which is a dark brown color. (Show picture of a Negroid family with lighter colored skin.) This Negroid family doesn't have as much melanin in their skin; therefore, their skin is lighter.

Physical characteristics of Negroid race:

1. Dark skin — because of the presence of melanin.
2. Woolly hair.
3. Short broad nose.
4. Protruding lower jaw.
5. Long legs in comparison to the trunk.

Physical characteristics of Mongoloid race:

1. Facial features smooth; nonprominent chin and brow.

2. Cheekbones jut forward.
3. Bridge of nose is low.
4. Eyes appear slanted because of skin which covers the inner eyelid.
5. Body build is stocky.
6. Legs are short.
7. Melanin is present in the skin—coloring is pale ivory to deep yellow brown.
8. Absence of almost any body hair.

Physical characteristics of Caucasoid race:

1. Stature varies from short to tall.
2. Body build is from slight to tall.
3. Nose form is varied, also mouth and lips.
4. Has facial hair.
5. A near lack of melanin in the skin in some groups.
6. A great deal of melanin in the skin of other groups.

Resources:

Questions: Pictures of Mongoloid and Caucasoid families. Do they all have the same amount of melanin in their skin? Which ones don't have as much melanin in their skin? How can you tell?

The Mongoloid race of people includes the American Indian, Eskimo, Chinese, Japanese, Hawaiian, mixed persons, etc.

The Caucasoid race is the classification give to Anglo-American, French, Danish, Russian, Swedish, German, mixed people, etc.

***Information taken from*:**

*_Teaching Children and Adults to Understand Human and Race Relations._ Grevious, Saundrah Black. Minneapolis, MN: T. S. Denison, 1968.

*_Prejudice and Your Child._ Black, Kenneth B. Boston, MA: Beacon Press, 1963.

*Excellent reference for the teacher.

PEOPLE ARE IMPORTANT (first grade)

Introduction

Teachers must realize their responsibilities to instill in the minds of the learners a respect for all people regardless of skin color, religion, nationality, or ancestry. It is the responsibility of the concerned teacher to destroy prejudices, biases, and harmful myths through meaningful learning situations.

INTEREST APPROACH

Leaves are beautiful
When Autumn changes them . . .
Red, brown and orange
Yellow and deep gold.

People are beautiful
In colors that distinguish them
Red, yellow, brown, pink
For young and old.

by Saundrah B. Grevious

I. Concept: Basic human needs and human dignity
Generalization: Human beings of all races show common likenesses and differences.

II. Behavioral Goals
   A. The learner will listen to stories and poems, see films, sing songs, examine pictures, listen to recordings and tapes and play games to see likenesses and differences of people.
   B. The learner will discuss the likenesses and differences of people.
   C. The learner will make booklets, compose chart lists, draw or point illustrations, label the illustrations, write stories, etc.

D. The learner will display pictures, illustrations, etc. on the bulletin boards.

E. The learner will share with other classrooms the results of some of the above activities such as songs learned, games played, bulletin boards made, etc.

III. Suggested Procedures for Teachers

A. Read a story such as *What Mary Jo Wanted* (a story about a little Afro-American girl in a typical middle-class family who wanted and got a puppy as a pet). After the story is read, a discussion such as this follows: Have you ever said anything like this, "I would rather have a dog than anything on earth"? Mary is much like you then, right?

B. On chalkboard begin to make a list of how learners are like Mary:

1. Likes pets
2. Sleeps
3. Has family
4. Has problems

Teacher: Ask learners if they can say this about all races. If they can agree with the chart developed by them, they may title the chart "We are alike." Teach a song "Just Like Me" or view a film such as "Robert and Father Visit the Zoo" (shows an Afro-American family in a middle-class neighborhood). Have learners cut magazine pictures that fit chart display. Include resource magazines such as *Ebony.*

C. Read a book such as *Bread and Jam for Frances* (about a little badger who doesn't like to eat anything but bread and jam until her mother refuses to give her other food). After discussing the story briefly, get into a discussion of things children like or dislike.

Make two charts similar to these: We Have Likes, We Have Dislikes:

Likes	*Dislikes*
Birthdays	War
Cars	Fighting
Love	Sickness
Beauty	
Fun	

Sing songs such as the "Little Indian Brave" (shows how a child of another race has fun).

D. The learner may draw pictures of some likes and dislikes etc.

E. Display a bulletin board labeled "We Were All Babies." The learner will interview the mother at home and ask her to tell him something about himself when he was a baby, such as, my hair was curly, Mama gave me a bottle. The learner will share his photo with the class members.

F. Use a filmstrip such as: "Robert Goes Shopping." Buy birthday gift for mother, or get background for discussion on things. All People Are Important. Have pictures of all races.

G. The teacher reads a story such as *Gabrielle and Selina*. Shows Caucasoid and Afro-American girls who live in the same neighborhood. The two girls learn to appreciate the need for and fun of being different. After the story is read, the teacher should draw a large circle on the chalkboard. Put one dot in for G and one for S. Add a dot for each child in the room and their family members.

Make charts like these two:

We Are Different From Others

1. Our homes (see outline of content)
2. Daddy's job (see outline of content)
3. Our church
4. Our racial names (see outline of content)
   a. Mongoloid
   b. Negroid
   c. Caucasoid

I Am Different From My Family
1. Name
2. Size
3. Likes and dislikes
4. Habits

Show a filmstrip such as *The American Indian Religion*. We must like all people despite differences.

H. Each learner makes a booklet entitled *I Am Different From My Family and Neighbors.* Each child will write a creative sentence on each page to go with his drawing. "I like to fish but Susie doesn't."

I. Ask about twins. Explain identical and fraternal twins. If possible, show pictures and read stories and poems about twins. Ask each child to point out his own picture and label it. Discuss brothers and sisters have differences.

J. Teacher displays colorful pictures of many things: Animals, people, objects, plants, etc. Ask what is your favorite animal. Why? Discuss picture on display. Bring out differences in size, shape, color, etc. Discuss why this is necessary. Conclude that differences are beautiful and necessary, and are fun and exciting. Collect several pictures of different racial families engaged in various activities. Ask questions about their picture to help children generalize that families enjoy doing things together.

Suggested questions:
What is this family doing together?
Do you think they are having fun?
Would you enjoy doing this with your family?
Have you ever done this with your family?
What things do you enjoy doing with your family?

Discuss several pictures using procedure above. The teacher may want an opportunity for writing a story "All Families Do Things Together" or create songs by putting words to music. Display several pictures representing each kind of family—Negroid, Mongoloid, and Caucasoid. The teacher may wish to discuss the classification of the people under each group and physical characteristics of each racial group.

Teacher: Yes all these people are alike in some ways (place men on chalk ledge). Who can find something else alike about these people?

Possible grouping by sets: size, age boys, girls, babies, women, children, clothing, color of skin, families, etc.

Each time a set is formed it is important that the children be asked to state how the people in their set are alike. Record all sets on chart or chalkboard. Play game until children can generalize that the people could be families and that these families are different sizes and different colors.

Teacher: What is alike in most of the families? Let's write a story about the families in our game.

Possible story:

There are many kinds of families.

Families are different sizes.
A family may have a daddy and a mother.
Some families have many children.
Some families are small.
Some families have no children.
Families love each other.
Families are good.

Teacher: What should our story be called?

Possible titles:
Families
People
Our People Story
Differences are Beautiful
Differences are Necessary
Differences are Fun and Exciting

To prove the above three statements to be valid, have the children draw two identical pictures of their house and yard. The learner will color the first one with only one color crayon. Have the learner color the second one realistically. Help the learner see the contrast between the two and appreciate the differences.

K. The learner should bring magazine pictures of people who are beautiful.

People from all races and professions should have pictures of all races available and display them with other learners if the learners do not bring such pictures. As a culminating activity, the learners should display these pictures on a bulletin board with a two-line title such as "People Are Important," "People Are Beautiful."

IV. Evaluations

A. Ask questions such as the following:

1. How are we alike?
2. How are we different?
3. Is it good for us to be different? Why?
4. What does the saying "Forsake not the old when a new friend you find" mean?

B. Sing songs, recite poems, read charts, dramatize stories, read and share bulletin board displays and booklets with other classrooms and parents.

References:

People Are Important. Evans, Eva. New York: Capital, 1951.
Gabrielle and Selina. Disbarats, Peter. New York.

GAMES

African Blindman's Bluff

Number players: 5 or more
Formation of circle with two blindfolded players inside, etc.
Action: One blindfolded player has two sticks which he must hit together often to tell where he is. Instruct him to keep his sticks low so the other blindfolded player, who is "it," will not be struck in the face if he runs into him. When "it" tags the stickman, that person becomes "it" and a new stickman is chosen.

African Handball

Number of players: 6 or more
Action: Players are divided into two equal teams. Game started by member of team tossing ball to one on his side. Object of team is to keep in possession of the ball.

American Indian Ball Race
American Indian Kick the Stick Relay
Japanese Tag
Our Colorful Neighborhoods

What is a neighbor? Where and how does he live? Do you need him?

"OUR COLORFUL NEIGHBORHOOD"

I. Concept: Respect and Interdependence
Generalization: Neighborhoods are different, yet dependent on one another. They are better known and appreciated if some of their landmarks are recognized and understood. People from racial groups have helped these neighborhoods.

II. Behavioral Goals:
   A. Learner will be able to illustrate and write one or two sentences about different kinds of neighborhoods.

B. Learner will choose and read stories about life in different neighborhoods.
C. Learner will illustrate, in cartoon fashion, important events from books read and films viewed in the unit study.
D. Learner will be able to complete a short, duplicated form on each person studied.
E. Learner will define and understand terms that describe the neighborhoods included in this unit.
F. Learner will be contributor in the evaluation by taking part in making a mural of neighborhoods and landmarks in them.

III. Suggested Procedure: Neighborhoods

A. Racially Mixed Neighborhoods

Teacher: We have been learning about our neighborhood, its helpers and landmarks. Look at these pictures (put helpers of mixed races on the flannel board or show a picture of a neighborhood—the teachers will have these prepared).

1. Do you have some of these people in your neighborhood?
2. How are these people alike?
3. How are they different?
   a. The work they do for us
   b. Their skin color
4. How do neighborhoods change?
   a. Physical—old buildings are torn down and repaired; more houses are built
   b. People—segregation, integration
5. How is this neighborhood like yours? How is it different?

Terms such as urban, suburban, rural, ghetto, should be discussed. This will lead into the study of the ghetto.

Activities:

1. Discuss whether changes in a neighborhood are good.
2. Make cardboard replicas of businesses and human people.
3. Show second filmstrip, *Robert's Family and Their Neighbors*.
4. This film will help students visualize the many elements which make up a neighborhood; the nature of a community; and the goods, services and recreational facilities the community provides. It will aid teachers in guiding students to an awareness of the similarities between families of all races. Other sound filmstrips that would be effective are *Neighborhoods are Different* and *Robert Goes to the Zoo*, etc.

B. Ghettos

Teacher: Show film *Anthony Lives in Watts*

1. What kind of neighborhood is this?
2. How is it like yours? How is it different?
3. Why do people stay in one part of a city?

Responses:

People live where they can find work.
People have like interests.
People feel welcome there.

4. Why do they sometimes become unhappy?

Discuss riots (Read excerpts from "Fill It Like It Is.")

5. Compare Watts with downtown Los Angeles —are these neighborhoods dependent on each other?

In the above discussion define these terms: ghetto, slum, riot, segregated, minority, majority, democracy.

Definition of Terms:

1. Ghetto—A neighborhood where all members are of one race, culture, or religion. This could be Afro-American, Jews, Irish, Chinese, German, etc.
2. Integrated—Make whole or complete by adding or bringing together.
3. Rural—Characteristic of the country, or country people.
4. Segregated—Set apart from others or from main group; isolated, compelled to time, go to school apart from other racial groups.
5. Slum—Heavily populated area in which housing and living conditions are extremely poor.
6. Suburban—Residential district on the outskirts of town —middle-class conservation.
7. Minority—The lessor part; less than one-half total.
8. Riot—Wild or violent disorder, confusion, or disturbance of the peace, by a number of persons assembled together.

An older ghetto can be seen in *Jung Lives In Harlem*. Discuss the following:

1. Differences between these two ghettos and names of them. Some neighborhoods are older than others. Changes take place.
2. The likenesses of these two.
3. Are there other races of people who live in ghettos? Who? (Germans, Jews, etc.)
4. How is a slum different from a ghetto?

Activities:

1. Draw pictures of these two ghettos showing likenesses and differences. Label each with one sentence about them.
2. Tell the meaning of two new words you have learned in these films.

C. Indian on reservation and in city
D. Mexican-American of Southwest

IV. Important People and Places
Suggested Procedure (continue use of bulletin board)
What is a name?
What are landmarks?
Landmarks are something named after people, community's way of honoring a person who did something important for his neighborhood.

A. Display picture of John F. Kennedy and Martin Luther King.
1. Do you know these men?
2. What did each of them do?
3. How are they different?
4. What happened to both of them?
5. Are the landmarks in their name?

Maybe we can find more about these men by listening to these records: *Black Image Maker, Martin Luther King*; *John F. Kennedy, Memorial Album.*

1. After records, fill worksheet on these two men.
2. Read life of the two men.

B. Mary MacLeod Bethune: Read *She Wanted to Read.* Show pictures and play records *Black Image Makers* and use pictures from Afro-American Portfolio on Mary MacLeod Bethune.

Discussion:

1. What did we learn about these people?
2. Why do you think there is a school?
3. Why do you think the school is in a mostly black neighborhood?

Activities:

1. Children may role play episodes of her life in helping her become an outstanding American. (Picking cotton, teaching reading, and talking to the President of the United States.)

C. Other landmarks, Minnehaha Falls. Show picture of the falls and read quote from Longfellow's *Song of Hiawatha.*

Activities:

1. Read and discuss poems to the children. The teacher could have displays of many blacks, Indians, Mexican-Americans, Orientals, white, and a few national landmarks just for interest. Encourage students to do research on their own.

V. Culminating Activity

List neighborhoods and community features—homes, schools, businesses, playgrounds, and landmarks, etc.

To help reinforce the idea of interdependence, put these features into a large mural. (This could be started early in the unit and continued as the unit progresses; could depict each kind of neighborhood studied.) Include people and families that were in the unit. Let the children put a title on the mural. Hopefully, their title would reflect unit concept.

VI. Evaluation

A. Are children able to contribute significantly to the culminating activity?
B. Do children recognize and understand terms in discussing neighborhoods?
C. Are the students able to recognize and value the contributions that people included in this unit have made to our country?
D. Do they realize their own neighborhood's depending on other neighborhoods?
E. Do they respect the way of life of people in neighborhoods different from their own?
F. Does the learner know that neighborhoods have their outstanding landmarks which should be respected by all?

Other units that can be developed from this one:

I. Likenesses and Difference in People
   A. Likenesses
      1. Need food
      2. Clothes
      3. Shelter
      4. Have families
      5. Work and play
   B. Differences
      1. Skin color
      2. Kinds of homes
      3. Feelings
      4. Personalities

II. Color
   A. What causes skin coloring?
   B. Color makes an interesting variety of people

III. History of American Indian
   A. Their interesting past
   B. Their contributions—food, medicine

IV. Contributions to History of our Country
   A. They have come from all races.
   B. Have helped build our country.

V. Human Relations
   A. Understanding ourselves
   B. Understanding others

VI. Other Neighborhoods
   A. Mexican-American
   B. Oriental
   C. Jewish, etc.

"This I Believe," A Testimony by Mrs. Glass or a Summary of her Teaching Philosophy

1. An excellent way for us as teachers to change our attitudes about the poverty community in which disadvantaged youth live and about the disadvantaged family is to take a walk with self and then immerse self in the community and discover the problems that impede successful education of these people. We must change our outlook toward teaching of disadvantaged youth wherever they are found.
2. When you know you love and when you care, you will share. If people don't know each other and have a human relationship with each other, then they will have a kind of fear. Strangeness is the thing that separates people.
3. Circumstances shape one's life. Teachers must understand composition of classroom.
4. Beauty is in the eyes of the beholder. We must help youth to discover beauty.
5. We must teach youth the importance of what's in a name.
6. We should expose youth to values (and desirable images) but we do not impose our values upon them.
7. All people are of different shades of brown — the Negro is the blackest shade of brown.
8. You + me + we = people.
   People, people, people
   People need people
   People love people
   People are alike
   People are different
9. When communities are bland and indifferent to reality, students are denied the privilege to know people of varied races and different cultures.
10. Acceptability depends upon contact and understanding. When people do not know each other, they have some kind of fear.
11. When the only goal worshiped in academic success is

formal learning, students are denied the opportunity to explore seriously their power to grow fully in ways of satisfaction and participation in an unpredictable world. Education is the real answer to today's problems. However, teaching experiences are often not relevant. *Example*: Often students are given a cut flower rather than the learning of how the flower grows. Given fish rather than taught how to fish.

12. We cannot teach people how to live until we know how they are living.
13. Nobody has taught until somebody has learned.
14. Teachers must make students like themselves better . . . help students develop an image of himself and learn the people that he models. The thing of image is very important. Learn how a child develops an image.
15. Teachers should assist students in discovering the beautiful and that there is something beautiful about everyone.
16. A good teacher is one who can secure interest, give clear understanding, and provide for subsequent use in thinking.
17. Parenting—the work or skill of a person, mother and/or father in rearing a child. The most important techniques of parenting are support, control, and punishment.

Bibliography

SELECTED SOURCES OF INFORMATION

Books

Holy Bible, The. King James Version. Psalms: Selected Verses throughout the Book, John 21: 15-18, and Song of Solomon 2:10-13. New York: American Bible Society, 1816.

Popenoe, Paul Bowman. *Modern Marriage.* New York: Macmillan, 1940.

Shivers, Dauphine and Webster, Hazel B. *Top Ladies of Distinction, Incorporated.* Houston, Texas: Met Printing, Incorporated, 1994.

Steen, Ralph. *Texas History.* Austin, Texas: Steck Company, 1948.

Upshaw, Leonard. "Upshaw, Gus, Ella and Descendants," in *Nacogdoches County Families.* Dallas, Texas: Curtis Media Corporation, 1985.

Winegarten, Ruthe. *Black Texas Women.* Austin, Texas: University of Texas Press, 1995.

Family Papers

Professor and Mrs. E. J. Campbell, Tyler, Texas

President Glass, Texas College, Tyler, Texas

Willie Lee Campbell Glass, Tyler, Texas

Interviews

Farr, Anita, by Jerry Holbert. Nacogdoches, Texas, SFASU, September 9, 1997.

Gibson, Robert, by Jerry Holbert. Nacogdoches, Texas, SFASU, September 9, 1997.

Glass, Willie Lee Campbell, by Patsy J. Hallman. Tyler, Texas, intermittent interviews, 1996 through 1998.

——— by Patsy J. Hallman, Nacogdoches, intermittent interviews, 1996 through 1998.

——— by Patsy J. Hallman and Gloria Durr. SFASU, Nacogdoches, Texas, November 3, 1996.

——— by Patsy J. Hallman and Jerry Holbert. Nacogdoches, Texas, January, l0, 1997.

——— by Bobbie Johnson. Tyler, Texas, October 9, 1985.

——— by LaVerne Madlock. Tyler, Texas, October 1996–May 1998.

Healey, Marie, by Patsy J. Hallman. Denton, Texas, June 8, 1997.

Lamb, Frankie, by Patsy J. Hallman, Miller Grove, Texas, August 15, 1950.

Madlock, LaVerne, by Patsy J. Hallman. Tyler, Texas, intermittent interviews, 1996–1998.

——— by Patsy J. Hallman. Nacogdoches, Texas, intermittent interviews, 1996–1998.

McMichael, Clarence, by Patsy J. Hallman. Nacogdoches, Texas, SFASU, November 10, 1997.

——— by Jerry Holbert. Nacogdoches, Texas, SFASU, September 9, 1997.

Simon, C. L., by Jerry Holbert. Nacogdoches, Texas, SFASU. September 9, 1997.

Stephens, Donnya, by Patsy J. Hallman. Nacogdoches, Texas, SFASU. April 20, 1997.

——— by Patsy J. Hallman. Nacogdoches, Texas, SFASU, October 10, 1997.

Tigner, Dorothy, by Jerry Holbert. Nacogdoches, Texas, SFASU, September 9, 1997.

Upshaw, Marion, by Jerry Holbert. Nacogdoches, Texas, SFASU, September 9, 1997.

——— by Patsy J. Hallman. Nacogdoches, Texas, SFASU, April 16, 1997.

Wade, Larry, by Jerry Holbert. Nacogdoches, Texas, SFASU, September 9, 1997.

Weatherall, Betty, by Gloria Durr. SFASU, Nacogdoches, Texas, March 1997.

Williams, Charles D., by Patsy J. Hallman. Nacogdoches, Texas, SFASU, April 16, 1997.

Williams, Charles D., by Jerry Holbert. Nacogdoches, Texas, SFASU, September 9, 1997.

Newspapers and Magazines

Abernethy, Francis Edward. "Professor E. J. Campbell 1877–1937." *The Daily Sentinel,* May 29, 1983.

Daily Sentinel, The, March 1, 1985. "Monument Dedication."

Hollingsworth, Skip. "Grande Dames." *Texas Monthly,* April 1990, pp. 114–123.

Jones, John Paul. "Willie Lee Glass." *The Bold Pioneer,* Winter 1994

Nute, Rita. *The University of Texas Health Center.* "Breast Diagnostic Center." Fall/Winter 1985–1986.

Redland Herald, The. May 29, 1983. "Well-known Educator is Named to Hall of Fame."

Smith County News, The. "Hall of Fame Honors Mrs. Glass." October 9, 1985.

Tyler Morning Telegraph. May 25, 1986. "Don't Give Up."

———. February 22, 1990. "Prospects Open for Black Women."

———. May 6, 1986. "Goodwill Store Opened."

———. September 23, 1988. "Strauss Praises Glass At People of Vision Dinner."

———. November 19, 1997. "Latest Honors Reflect Well on Mrs. Glass, Tyler."

Tyler Courier-Times. November 29, 1976. "Great Trees from Small Acorns Grow."

———. November 29, 1976. "Developing Self-Images Vital to Tyler Woman."

———. February 16, 1986. "Civic Duties Call Local Leaders."

———. November 29, 1992. "Reception for Coretta Scott King."

———. April 27, 1986. "Celebrate Texas."

———. November 24, 1985. "Willie Lee Glass."

———. October 1, 1985. "Tyler Woman Hall of Fame Inductee."

———. November 21, 1985. "Walk with Willie Glass."

———. November 20, 1985. "A Special Day for Willie Lee."

———. May 10, 1985. "Mrs. Willie Glass Recognized."

Official Documents

RESOLUTION. H.R. No. 243. Austin, Texas: The State of Texas House of Representatives, February 27, 1997.

SENATE RESOLUTION. S.R. No. 257. Austin, Texas: The Senate, February 27, 1997.

Programs (examples selected from family papers)

E. J. Campbell Professorship in Educational Leadership. Nacogdoches, Texas. Stephen F. Austin State University. September 9, 1997.

East Texas Communities Foundation, *3rd Annual Philanthropy Day Awards Luncheon,* Tyler, November 19, 1997.

Honors and Awards Ceremony. Ames, Iowa: Iowa State University Alumni Association, October 24, 1997.

Recognition Soiree Honoring Mrs. Willie Lee Dorothy Campbell Glass. Martin Hall, Texas College, Tyler, Texas, November 17, 1974.

Sketches

Aberle, Catalina. SFASU Student in HMS 233, 1997. "Basketball Uniform Sketch."

Burk, Jinger. SFASU Student in HMS 233, 1997. "Wedding Dress Sketch."

Kriel, Andre, "Cover Sketch," 1998.

Unpublished Manuscripts

Brownlee, Laura. "Willie Lee Glass, East-T-Plex Living Legend." Tyler, Texas: Combined Underwriters Life Insurance Company, 1986.

Durr, Gloria Ebarb. "Nomination for Distinguished Achievement Citation. Ames, Iowa: Iowa State University Alumni Association. 1997

Glass, Willie Lee. "Mental Fashions for the Seventies." Lubbock, Texas: Texas Tech University, June 1970.

——— "Teacher-in-Service Workshops and Conferences," January-December 1972.

——— "Curriculum Materials." 1970s.

Kenner, Janie, Ph.D. "Willie Lee Glass: A Lady of Remarkable Style." Nacogdoches, Texas: Stephen F. Austin State University, June 5, 1995.

University Bulletins

Iowa State University, 1997.

Prairie View A&M University, 1997.

Texas College Bulletin, 1997.

Virginia State College Bulletin, 1997.

Video

The Texas Women's Hall of Fame. Wimberley, Texas: Southwest Media Services, Inc. 1985.

About the Author

Mrs. Glass' story was written by PATSY JOHNSON HALLMAN, associate dean, College of Education, Stephen F. Austin State University (SFASU). She holds degrees from Texas A&M, Commerce, SFASU, and Texas Woman's University. She taught public schools in Texas (K-12) and has been at SFASU since 1970 in the roles of professor of home economics education and as associate dean for teacher education, College of Education. Her research interests have focused on curriculum development.

Patsy Hallman has been an admirer of Mrs. Glass since they met in 1951 at a state meeting of Future Homemakers of America. At the time Mrs. Glass was the new Texas Education Agency consultant, and the author was a high school student. Years later their paths crossed as they served together on a State Curriculum Committee.

The opportunity to write the Glass/Campbell story came as a result of the establishment of the EJ Campbell Professorship in Educational Leadership at Stephen F. Austin State University. Ms. Hallman was asked by a committee at SFASU to develop the manuscript. She has been pleased to work with Mrs. Glass and Mrs. LaVerne Madlock to review references and interview friends and acquaintances in order to write the story.

Ms. Hallman and her husband, Dr. Leon Hallman, live in Nacogdoches.